Fam Breaks in Britain

2010

THG UPERARD

Family Holiday and Days Out Guide

including Britain's Blue Flag Beaches

© FHG Guides Ltd, 2010
ISBN 978-1-85055-427-1

Maps: ©MAPS IN MINUTES™ / Collins Bartholomew (2009)

Typeset by FHG Guides Ltd, Paisley.
Printed and bound in China by Imago.

Distribution. Book Trade: ORCA Book Services, Stanley House,
3 Fleets Lane, Poole, Dorset BH15 3AJ
Tel: 01202 665432; Fax: 01202 666219
e-mail: mail@orcabookservices.co.uk

Published by FHG Guides Ltd., Abbey Mill Business Centre,
Seedhill, Paisley PA1 ITJ
Tel: 0141-887 0428; Fax: 0141-889 7204
e-mail: admin@fhguides.co.uk

Family Breaks in Britain is published by FHG Guides Ltd,
part of Kuperard Group.

Cover design: FHG Guides
Cover Picture: Fylde Borough Council

Acknowledgements: Our thanks for pictures courtesy of:

Isle of Wight Council (p10)
Visit Cornwall (p12, 15)
English Riviera Tourist Board (p8, 40); Woodlands Leisure Park (p30)
The Big Sheep (p43)
The Milky Way Adventure Park (p44)
Visit Wiltshire (p52)
Poole Tourism (p60, 66); Poole Tourism, photo taken by Reefoto (p1, 62)
Eastbourne Borough Council (p76, 78)
Thanet District Council (p81)
Leighton Buzzard Railway (p92)
Heritage Motor Centre (p99)
National Railway Museum (p110)
Scarborough Borough Council (p112)
Fylde Borough Council (p118); The World of Glass (p122)
Blackpool Tourism (p119)
VisitScotland (p130, 133, 142)
Cardiff County Council (p152)

Contents

Readers' Offer Vouchers	163-180
Good Beach Guide	8-11
CORNWALL	12
SOUTH DEVON	30
NORTH DEVON	43
SOMERSET AND WILTSHIRE	52
HAMPSHIRE AND DORSET	60
ISLE OF WIGHT	72
SUSSEX	76
KENT	81
LONDON & HOME COUNTIES	86
EAST OF ENGLAND (Bedfordshire, Cambridgeshire, Essex, Hertfordshire, Norfolk, Suffolk)	92
MIDLANDS (Derbyshire, Gloucestershire Herefordshire, Leicestershire, Lincolnshire, Northamptonshire, Nottinghamshire, Oxfordshire, Shropshire, Staffordshire, Warwickshire, West Midlands, Worcestershire)	99
NORTH EAST ENGLAND (Durham, Northumberland, Tyne & Wear, Yorkshire)	110
NORTH WEST ENGLAND (Cheshire, Cumbria, Greater Manchester, Lancashire, Merseyside)	118
SCOTLAND	130
WALES	147
Index of Towns/Regions	181

enjoy a family break at one of Darwin's award winning holiday parks across the beautiful South West

The range of facilities include*
- ☑ Lodges & Holiday Homes
- ☑ Grass Camping Pitches
- ☑ Fully Serviced Caravan Pitches
- ☑ Motor Home Facilities
- ☑ Pools, Activities & Playgrounds
- ☑ Seasonal Pitches
- ☑ Shops, Bars & Restaurants
- ☑ Family Entertainment
- ☑ Transport Links

special offers & discounts online — Pet Friendly

🌐 www.darwinholidays.co.uk
✉ enquiries@darwinholidays.co.uk

darwin holiday parks

Win Getting out with your family is important and even if you have a little one to carry around why don't you try the holiday product of choice – **theBabaSling**™. It makes life much more spontaneous enabling mum, dad, grandparents or even friends to keep the baby happy and safe whilst joining in the fun of the holiday.

Walking and taking in the beautiful countryside or seaside is hassle free with **theBabaSling**™.
Simply use the sling on your front, back or side leaving your hands free to take the holiday snaps or keep the dog on a lead and away from those unsuspecting sheep!

It's a great solution for limited caravan or car boot storage space, leaving you more room for toys, games and clothes. **theBabaSling**™ can be used from birth until toddler, is very comfortable to wear, and has seven natural carrying positions.

Available in seven cheery colours and costing only £49.90 makes it the perfect holiday essential whatever the destination.

www.theBabaSling.co.uk

You can win one of these by answering this simple question:
How many different carrying positions does **theBabaSling**™ have?

Name...

Address ....

....

Postcode ....Date.....................................

 To enter, cut out this slip and return to FHG GUIDES LTD, ABBEY MILL BUSINESS CENTRE, SEEDHILL, PAISLEY PA1 1TJ
Closing date JULY 30th 2010

A sign of excellence.
Just one of 200 superb Caravan Club Sites to choose from

Broomfield Farm Caravan Club Site

Caravan Club Sites are renowned for their excellence. With most of those graded achieving 4 or 5 stars from VisitBritain, you can be sure of consistently high standards. From lakes or mountains to city or sea, there are some 200 quality Club Sites throughout Britain & Ireland to choose from.

With over 40 fabulous Club Sites open all year, why stay at home?

Whichever site you choose, you can be assured of excellent facilities and a friendly welcome from our Resident Wardens. Just look for the signs.

Bunree Caravan Club Site

Burrs Country Park Caravan Club Site

Troutbeck Head Caravan Club Site

Touring Britain & Ireland
The Caravan Club Site Collection

You don't have to be a member to stay on most Caravan Club Sites, but members save up to £7 per night on pitch fees!

Call today for your FREE Touring Britain & Ireland brochure on 0800 521 161 quoting FHG10
or visit www.caravanclub.co.uk

The Caravan Club, East Grinstead House, East Grinstead, West Sussex RH19 1UA

England and Wales • Counties

1. Plymouth
2. Torbay
3. Poole
4. Bournemouth
5. Southampton
6. Portsmouth
7. Brighton & Hove
8. Medway
9. Thurrock
10. Southend
11. Slough
12. Windsor & Maidenhead
13. Bracknell Forest
14. Wokingham
15. Reading
16. West Berkshire
17. Swindon
18. Bath & Northeast Somerset
19. North Somerset
20. Bristol
21. South Gloucestershire
22. Luton
23. Milton Keynes
24. Peterborough
25. Leicester
26. Nottingham
27. Derby
28. Telford & Wrekin
29. Stoke-on-Trent
30. Warrington
31. Halton
32. Merseyside
33. Blackburn with Darwen
34. Blackpool
35. N.E. Lincolnshire
36. North Lincolnshire
37. Kingston-upon-Hull
38. York
39. Redcar & Cleveland
40. Middlesborough
41. Stockton-on-Tees
42. Darlington
43. Hartlepool

NORTH WALES
a. Denbighshire
b. Flintshire
c. Wrexham

SOUTH WALES
d. Swansea
e. Neath & Port Talbot
f. Bridgend
g. Rhondda Cynon Taff
h. Merthyr Tydfil
i. Vale of Glamorgan
j. Cardiff
k. Caerphilly
l. Blaenau Gwent
m. Torfaen
n. Newport
o. Monmouthshire

Guide to Good Beaches

How can I find a good, clean beach?
Can I take my dog on the beach?
How do I know the water is safe to swim in?

Britain has hundreds of beautiful beaches, many peaceful and secluded, others with lots of facilities which make them popular with families.
There are five beach scheme awards, and if you contact them or have a look at their websites, you will find lots of information on what is the best one for you and your family.

Started in 1987 as part of the EEC's Year of the Environment, the **BLUE FLAG** campaign aims not only to encourage and reward high standards of beach management at coastal resorts, but also to promote improved quality of bathing water. It is awarded in over 41 countries in Europe, South Africa, Morocco, Tunisia, New Zealand, Brazil, Canada and the Caribbean to resort beaches and marinas with high standards  of environmental management. To win a Blue Flag, therefore, water quality is judged along with cleanliness and beach facilities. A dog ban during the summer is an absolute requirement and only beaches regularly used by the public, and resorts with safe bathing all year round may enter the competition. In 2009 99 beaches in Britain were awarded the coveted Blue Flag Award. Keep Britain Tidy co-ordinates the scheme in England, while Keep Scotland Tidy, Keep Wales Tidy and Tidy Northern Ireland oversee the scheme in their respective countries.

Keep Britain Tidy administers the Quality Coast Awards in England. The award-winning beaches have met very strict criteria, which include meeting the EC requirements for bathing water, providing good beach safety and supervision, putting in place good beach management (including dog controls and facilities for disabled visitors) and providing the public with clear information. A large database of UK beaches is maintained, with information on water quality, access, safety, cleanliness, dog control, first aid provision and conservation management.

In Scotland, Wales and Northern Ireland, **Seaside Awards** are presented annually for well maintained and managed resort and rural beaches, where bathing water quality must achieve the EC mandatory standard.

Green Coast Award is run by Keep Wales Tidy and is given to unspoilt rural beaches in Wales and the Republic of Ireland for high water quality and best practice in environmental management. It places a great emphasis on community and environmental activities, and is intended to promote and protect rural beaches. Bathing water must achieve the EC Guideline standard.

The Marine Conservation Society produces a list of 'recommended' beaches which have the highest standards of bathing water quality. This award only addresses water quality and lists beaches which pose a minimum risk of sewage contamination and related diseases.

The Good Beach Guide (online www.goodbeachguide.co.uk) is a searchable database of beaches in the UK and Ireland, each with description, photo and map. In 2009 370 beaches were 'MSC Recommended' for excellent water quality.

How to find out more:
Blue Flag Beaches • www.blueflag.org.uk
Quality Coast Awards • www.keepbritaintidy.org
Seaside Awards • www.keepscotlandbeautiful.org
Green Coast Award • www.keepwalestidy.org
Marine Conservation Society • www.mcsuk.org

Guide to Good Beaches

Family fun on the Isle of Wight

Cornwall
Carbis Bay
Gyllyngvase
Polzeath
Porthmeor
Porthtowan
Sennen Cove

North Devon
Ilfracombe Tunnels
Westward Ho!
Woolacombe Sands

South Devon
Bigbury on Sea
Blackpool Sands
Challaborough
Dawlish Warren
Torbay
  Breakwater
  Broadsands
  Meadfoot
  Oddicombe

Dorset
Bournemouth
  Fisherman's Walk
  Alum Chine
  Durley Chine
  Southbourne
Poole
  Canford Cliffs
  Branksome Chine
  Sandbanks
  Shore Road
Swanage Central

Hampshire
Hayling Island Central
Hayling Island West

Sussex
Littlehampton Coastguards
West Wittering
West Street

Kent
Birchington Minnis Bay
Botany Bay
Joss Bay
St Mildred's Bay
Ramsgate Main Sands
West Bay Westgate

Isle of Wight
Sandown
Ventnor

Norfolk
Cromer
Mundesley
Sea Palling
Sheringham

Essex
Brightlingsea
Clacton-on-Sea
Dovercourt
Shoebury Common
Shoeburyness
Three Shells

Suffolk
Felixstowe South
Lowestoft North
Lowestoft South

Lincolnshire
Cleethorpes Central
Mablethorpe Central
Skegness Central
Sutton on Sea Central

Guide to Good Beaches

Tyne & Wear
Roker
Sandhaven
Tynemouth
  King Edwards Bay
  Longsands South
Whitley Bay South

East Yorkshire
Bridlington North
Hornsea

North Yorkshire
Scarborough North
Whitby

WALES

Gwynedd
Abermaw
Abersoch
Barmouth
Dinas Dinlle
Fairbourne
Pwllheli
Rhos-on-Sea/Colwyn Bay
Tywyn
Victoria Dock

Anglesey
Benllech
Church Bay
Llanddona
Llanddwyn
Newborough
Porth Dafarch

North Wales
Prestatyn Central

Ceredigion
Aberystwyth North
Aberystwyth South
New Quay

Carmarthenshire
Pendine

Pembrokeshire
Broadhaven North
Dale
Lydstep
Newgale
Newport
Poppit Sands
Saundersfoot
St Davids Whitesands
Tenby North
Tenby South

South Wales
Bracelet Bay
Caswell Bay
Langland Bay
Porthcawl Rest Bay
Port Eynon

SCOTLAND

Dundee & Angus
Broughty Ferry
Montrose

Fife
Aberdour Silver Sands
Burntisland
St Andrews West
Elie (Woodhaven)

NORTHERN IRELAND

Benone
Cranfield
Murlough
Portrush White Rocks
Portstewart
Tyrella

Cornwall

CORNWALL

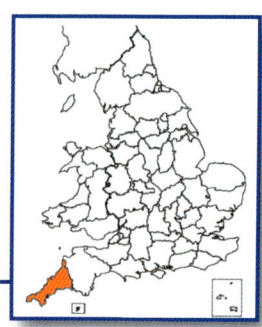

Best Beaches

Several beaches which meet the strict criteria of the European Foundation for Environmental Education have been awarded a prestigious Blue Flag.

BLUE FLAG BEACHES 2009
- Polzeath
- Carbis Bay
- St Ives Porthmeor
- Sennen Cove
- Gyllyngvase
- Porthtowan

 South West Tourism
(Bristol & Bath, Cornwall, Devon, Dorset, Gloucestershire & The Cotswolds, Somerset, Wiltshire).
- **Tel: 0870 442 0880**
- **Fax: 0870 442 0881**
- **e-mail: info@swtourism.org.uk**
- **www.visitsouthwest.co.uk**

Porthminster Beach, St Ives

For more information about holidaying in Cornwall see: www.visitcornwall.com
- www.cata.co.uk (Cornwall Association of Tourist Attractions) • www.secta.org.uk (S.E. Cornwall)
- www.north-cornwall.com (North Cornwall) • www.go-cornwall.com (West Cornwall)

Cornwall

BUDE

Family Fun Activities: Seawater swimming pool on Summerleaze beach • Tropical Leisure Pool, including flume and wave machine, fitness suite, 10-pin bowling, roller blading rink and indoor adventure play area • Adventure centres offering tuition in various sports • Sports hall, multi-gym and activities • Sustrans cycle route • Bude Canal Wharf area • Heritage Trail • Museum • Mini-golf, putting, golf, bowls, squash, table tennis, cricket, tennis, sea and canal angling.

Special Events: May: Model Boat Festival; re-enactment of Battle of Stamford Hill. **May-September:** events, shows, fetes and revels. **July:** Bude festival of Music, Downhill Classic Triathlon. **August:** arts & crafts exhibitions; Bude Carnival Week; Lifeboat Week; 8-day Bude Jazz Festival. **September:** Quadrathon. **October:** canoe sprint.

Bude Visitor Centre, The Crescent, Bude EX23 8LE • 01288 354240
e-mail: budetic@visitbude.info
www.visitbude.info

Beaches

• **SUMMERLEAZE BEACH.** Level access via car park. *Safety and maintenance:* lifeguards during summer months. *Beach facilities:* beach huts, deck chairs etc for hire; mini-golf and go karts; open sea pool; cafe, shop and restaurant; RNLI centre/shop. Toilets, & access. *Dog restrictions:* none, but they must be kept under proper control.

• **CROOKLETS BEACH.** Sandy, with level access. Car park adjoining. *Safety and maintenance:* lifeguards on duty during June/July/August. *Beach facilities:* deckchairs, beach huts, windbreaks etc for hire; snack bar and beach shop; toilets (disabled facilities for members of National Radar Key Scheme). *Dog restrictions:* banned from beach area from Good Friday to 1st October.

• **SANDY MOUTH BEACH.** Beach owned by National Trust. *Safety and maintenance:* lifeguards during summer months. *Beach facilities:* cafe owned by NT. Toilets but no & facilities. *Dog restrictions:* none.

NEWQUAY

Family Fun Activities: Tunnels Through Time • Dairyland • Cornwall Pearl • Trerice Manor • Trenance Park with Water World fun pool and Newquay Zoo • Blue Reef Aquarium • Tennis, golf, pitch and putt, miniature railway, lakeside cafe, boating, sailing, surfing (Fistral Beach), angling, golf course • Discos, nightclubs.

Special Events: June: Newquay Surf Triathlon. **July:** Surf Festival, Newquay Harbour Sports. **August:** British Surfing Championships. Gig racing.

Tourist Information Centre, Marcus Hill, Newquay • 01637 854020
www.newquay.org.uk

Beaches

• **HARBOUR BEACH.** Sandy and naturally sheltered; promenade and limited parking. *Safety and maintenance:* cleaned daily. *Beach facilities:* pleasure craft; fishing and shark trips; ice cream kiosk; restaurant; toilets with & access.

• **TOWAN BEACH.** 400 yards long, sandy with rock pools, naturally sheltered promenade. & access. Parking 5 minutes' walk. *Safety and maintenance:* flagged, warning signs, lifeguards; cleaned daily. *Beach facilities:* deck chairs, windbreaks, wet suits; ice-cream kiosk, snack bar.

• **GREAT WESTERN BEACH.** 200 yards long, sandy with rock pools and cliffs; parking 5 minutes' walk. *Safety and maintenance:* flagged, warning signs, lifeguards; cleaned daily. *Beach facilities:* deck chairs, windbreaks, surfboards; ice cream and snack bar; toilets with & access.

Cornwall

- **TOLCARNE BEACH.** 500 yards long, sandy. Access down cliff steps, also path to beach. Parking 6 minutes' walk. *Safety and maintenance:* flagged, warning signs; cleaned daily. *Beach facilities:* deck chairs, surfboards, beach huts, trampolines; ice-cream kiosks, cafeteria, beach shop, barbecues; toilets.

- **LUSTY GLAZE BEACH.** 200 yards long; sandy with cliffs and rock pools, access via steps. *Safety and maintenance:* flagged, warning signs, lifeguards; cleaned daily. *Beach facilities:* deck chairs, surf boards, beach huts; ice-cream kiosk, cafe/takeaway, pub/restaurant and beach shop; showers and toilets; outdoor adventure centre. *Dog restrictions:* banned between 8am and 7pm.

- **PORTH BEACH.** 300 yards long, sandy and naturally sheltered with rock pools. Good parking. *Safety and maintenance:* flagged, warning signs, lifeguards; cleaned daily. *Beach facilities:* deck chairs, boogie boards, windbreaks; ice-cream kiosks, snack bars, restaurant and pub. *Dog restrictions:* banned from Easter to end September.

- **WHIPSIDERRY BEACH.** 200 yards long; sandy with cliffs and steps. *Safety and maintenance:* warning signs; cut off by tidal seas around cliffs.

- **WATERGATE BEACH.** Two miles long, sandy; good parking. *Safety and maintenance:* flagged, warning signs, lifeguards; cleaned daily. *Beach facilities:* surfboards; surf school and power kite school; bistro and takeaway, shops; toilets.

- **CRANTOCK BEACH.** Approx. one mile long, naturally sheltered with sandy dunes; good parking. *Safety and maintenance:* flagged, warning signs, lifeguards; Gannel tidal estuary very dangerous when tide going out. Beach owned and cleaned by NT. *Beach facilities:* deck chairs, surf boards, ice-cream kiosks, snack bars; toilets.

- **FISTRAL BEACH.** Approx. one mile long, sandy with dunes; good parking. *Safety and maintenance:* flagged, warning signs, lifeguards; cleaned daily. *Beach facilities:* deck chairs and windbreaks; wetsuit and surfboard hire; restaurant, cafe and takeaway, shops; toilets with ♿ access.

PENZANCE

Family Fun Activities: Water sports area at Marazion • Sea water swimming pool, indoor swimming pool, children's playground, boating lake, amusement arcade • Riding, tennis, bowls, putting, go-karting • Shark fishing, sailing, sub-aqua, sea and fresh water angling • Rock climbing • Cinema, arts theatre, dance halls and discos, clubs and pub entertainment nightly.

Special Events: April: British Funboard Cup, Hockey Festival. **June:** Golowan Festival. **August:** Newlyn Fish Festival. **September:** Michaelmas Fair.

Tourist Information Centre,
Station Road, Penzance TR18 2NF
01736 362207
www.go-cornwall.com

ST IVES

Family Fun Activities: Boat trips, sea angling, sailing, surfing, parascending, tennis, bowling, squash, putting • Leisure centre with swimming pool and gym • Museum, art galleries (Tate St Ives).

Tourist Information Centre,
The Guildhall, St Ives TR26 2DS
01736 796297
www.visit-westcornwall.com

Beaches

- **PORTHMEOR BEACH.** One km long, sand backed by low cliffs. Good surfing beach. Limited parking. *Safety and maintenance:* area for use of surfboards marked with buoys, lifeguards in summer months; cleaned daily during holiday season. *Beach facilities:* deck chairs, surf boards, beach huts for hire; boat trips around bay; beach shop and cafe on promenade; toilets. *Dog restrictions:* banned from Easter to 1st October.

Cornwall

☆ Fun for all the Family ☆

◆ **Colliford Lake Park, Bolventnor, Bodmin (01208 821469).** Set amidst 50 acres of moorland beauty, rare breeds of animals and birds, craft demonstrations, Kids' Kingdom all-weather playground.
www.collifordlakepark.co.uk

◆ **Dairyland Farmworld, near Newquay (01872 510246).** An all-weather attraction with fun for the whole family. Mini tractors, trampolines, assault course, farm park, pony rides, and lots, lots more
www.dairylandfarmworld.com

◆ **Futureworld@Goonhilly, near Helston (0800 679593).** From Cold War technology to the Apple iPhone, a wide variety of fun and interactive displays for all ages. Segway tours, cafe.
www.goonhilly.bt.com

◆ **Lappa Valley Railway and Leisure Park, St Newlyn East, Newquay (01872 510317).** Two-mile ride on steam train, plus leisure area with crazy golf, adventure playground, boating lake, picnic areas, woodland walks.
www.lappavalley.co.uk

◆ **The Monkey Sanctuary, near Looe (01503 262532).** Breeding colony of "Woolly" monkeys that enjoy the company of visitors!
www.monkeysanctuary.org

◆ **Newquay Zoo, Trenance Gardens, Newquay (01637 873342).** A wealth of wildlife including Tropical House, Children's Zoo, walk in Rabbit Warren; play areas; park with leisure facilities.
www.newquayzoo.org.uk

◆ **Paradise Park, near Hayle (01736 751020).** Cornwall's conservation theme park which keeps and breeds endangered species.
www.paradisepark.org.uk

◆ **Poldark Mine and Heritage Complex, Wendron, Helston (01326 573173).** An 18th century Cornish tin mine at 125 feet below ground level. Guided tours and working models; restaurant.
www.poldark-mine.co.uk

◆ **Tamar Otter Wildlife Centre, near Launceston (01566 785646).** Enjoy a close encounter with these shy but playful creatures; also deer, owls and golden pheasants. Nature trail, tearoom and shop. No dogs.
www.tamarotters.co.uk

◆ **Tunnels Through Time, Newquay (01637 873379).** More than 70 amazingly realistic characters re-create the stories and legends of Cornwall. Open Easter-October.
www.tunnelsthroughtime.co.uk

Lappa Valley Steam Railway

POLURRIAN HOTEL

Set in 12 acres of secluded gardens with stunning views across Mount's Bay.

The hotel has both an indoor and outdoor swimming pool, snooker room, children's play area, tennis court, sun terraces and new Purity Treatment Rooms offering Elemis and Spieza 100% organic.

Most of the recently refurbished bedrooms have sea views and all have baby listening facilities.

Our restaurant offers excellent food in stylish surroundings with stunning views.

Mullion, Lizard Peninsula,
Cornwall TR12 7EN
Tel: 01326 240421 • Fax: 01326 240083
e-mail: relax@polurrianhotel.com
www.polurrianhotel.com

Cornwall

•Sunrise•
6 Burn View, Bude EX23 8BY
Tel: 01288 353214
Fax: 01288 359911
sunriseguest@btconnect.com
www.sunrise-bude.co.uk

Sunrise offers something special... with Four Stars and a Silver Award to prove it. Immaculate en suite accommodation providing comfort, style and service with a smile. Superb breakfasts and ideal location, opposite golf club, close to shops, restaurants and pubs. Travel cot and high chair available. Ideal for short or long stays. Evening meals by arrangement. Highly recommended.

LANGFIELD MANOR
Broadclose, Bude, Cornwall EX23 8DP

- Quality apartments within fine Edwardian house, sleep 2-6.
- Games room with snooker, pool and table tennis tables.
- 3 minutes' walk to shops and beautiful sandy beaches.
- Peacefully situated in delightful, sheltered south-facing gardens.
- Heated outdoor swimming pool.
- Golf course adjacent.
- Open all year.
- Terms from £280 per week.

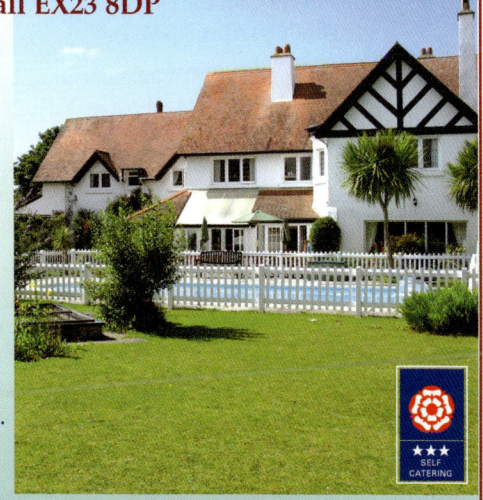

Tel: 01288 352415
langfieldmanor@btconnect.com
www.langfieldmanor.co.uk

Penrose Burden Holiday Cottages

St Breward, Bodmin, Cornwall PL30 4LZ
Tel: 01208 850277 / 850617 • Fax: 01208 850915

Penrose Burden is the perfect place to relax, unwind and leave behind the pressures of modern life. Situated in North Cornwall and perched on the very edge of the majestic Bodmin Moor, which extends to over 100 square miles, it is surely one of the last completely unspoilt places in England. Its central location makes both coastlines easily accessible; the South with its long sandy beaches, historic ports, secluded creeks and the Eden Project, and the North with its dramatic cliffs, quiet coves, grand country houses and historic market towns.

Traditional stone buildings have been carefully converted to single level self-catering cottages and sympathetically designed with the needs of wheelchair users in mind. Exposed beams and original features blend well with walls hung with original paintings by local artists and simple modern furnishings. Each has a wood-burning stove with plentiful logs for year-round comfort, their own private garden, and outstanding views over our wooded valley and beyond to the dramatic moorland.

Easy access to some of the country's best surfing beaches, dinghy sailing, wind surfing, horse riding on the Moor, free salmon or trout fishing on our own mile of river bank, swimming and tennis (at the nearby country house hotel by arrangement), bike riding on The Camel Trail, or a game of golf on any one of the area's four golf courses.

...just peace, tranquillity and space to relax

Please write or telephone for a colour brochure.   Nancy Hall

www.penroseburden.co.uk

Cornwall

 **Caravan and Camping Park**

Bude, Cornwall EX23 0LP
Tel: 01288 352017 • Fax: 01288 359034
e-mail: reception@upperlynstone.co.uk • www.upperlynstone.co.uk

Upper Lynstone is a quiet family-run park situated just three-quarters of a mile from Bude's town centre on the coastal road to Widemouth Bay. Bude's shops, beaches with outdoor pool, bars and restaurants are all within walking distance.

Enjoy the breathtaking beauty of the Cornish Coast from the footpath that leads from our park. The park has modern caravans for hire and spacious camping and touring fields with electric hook-ups. Facilities include a small but well equipped shop, free showers, laundry room, and children's play area. Calor and Camping Gas stockists. Well-behaved dogs welcome.

We have four and six berth caravans at Upper Lynstone. All have mains services, colour TV, fridge etc. The caravans are well spaced with plenty of room for you to park. They have splendid views to distant villages and moors. Enjoy our NEW 35ft, 3-bedroom static caravans with panoramic views, designed to sleep six in comfort.

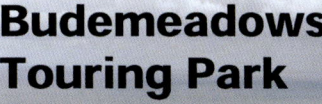

Budemeadows Touring Park

Widemouth Bay,
Bude, Cornwall. EX23 0NA
☎ 01288 361646   📠 08707 064825

A friendly family-run site in landscaped surroundings just 3 miles from Bude and a mile from Widemouth Bay.

✓ Heated Pool
✓ Children's Playgrounds
✓ Grumpy Pete's Bar
✓ Licensed Shop
✓ Laundrette
✓ Free Hot Water and Showers

Please ring or e-mail for a brochure.
Pool, bar and shop open mid and high season

Open all year
✉ holiday@budemeadows.com
🌐 www.budemeadows.com

Hilton Farm Holiday Cottages
Marhamchurch, Bude EX23 0HE
Tel & Fax: 01288 361521

Where coast meets countryside, in an Area of Outstanding Natural Beauty, the ideal place to make the most of Devon and Cornwall. Superb setting in 25 acres of ground. 16th century farmhouse, sleeps 10; three new luxury cottages and six fully equipped converted barn cottages. Superb heated outdoor swimming pool and jacuzzi, all-weather tennis court, activity area/play area/barbecue and picnic area; laundry facilities. Just two miles from sandy beaches; world-famous Eden Project 45 minutes' drive. Self-catering cottages open all year.
Contact: Fiona & Ian Goodman.

e-mail: ian@hiltonfarmhouse.freeserve.co.uk
www.hiltonfarmholidays.co.uk

Sheltered, peaceful family park on the stunning north Cornish coastline.

In a sheltered spot, within an area of Outstanding Natural Beauty, Hentervene offers a friendly, safe environment for the family. Moments from the award-winning beach at Crackington Haven, with its rock pools, sand, and surf, and life guards in main season. Lovely beach café.

Hentervene offers the perfect environment for the perfect holiday. Whether you choose to stay in one of our modern caravans or a luxury lodge, Hentervene has everything you need. Peace and tranquillity for that stress-free, relaxing holiday.
You can be confident that our facilities are clean and well maintained.

Lots more information and reviews on our website.

Hentervene Caravan Park, Crackington Haven
Near Bude EX23 0LF • 01840 230365
e-mail: contact@hentervene.co.uk • www.hentervene.co.uk

Creekside Cottages • Cornwall

31 Exclusive Holiday Cottages in South Cornwall

A fine selection of individual water's edge, village and rural cottages, sleeping from 2-10, situated around the creeks of the Carrick Roads, near Falmouth, South Cornwall. Set in enchanting and picturesque positions, with many of the cottages offering panoramic creek views. Perfect locations for family holidays, all close to superb beaches, extensive sailing and boating facilities, Cornish gardens and excellent walks. The majority of the cottages are available throughout the year, and all offer peaceful, comfortable and fully equipped accommodation; most have open fires. Dogs welcome.

Just come and relax

For a colour brochure please phone **01326 375972**
www.creeksidecottages.co.uk

Fowey Harbour Cottages

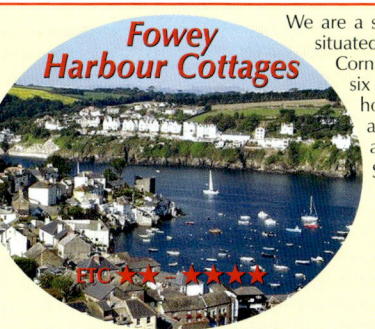

We are a small Agency offering a selection of cottages and flats situated around the beautiful Fowey Harbour on the South Cornish Coast. Different properties accommodate from two to six persons and vary in their decor and facilities so that hopefully there will be something we can offer to suit anyone. All properties are registered with VisitBritain and are personally vetted by us.

Short Breaks and weekend bookings accepted subject to availability (mainly out of peak season but sometimes available at "last minute" in season).

**Brochure and details from W. J. B. Hill & Son,
3 Fore Street, Fowey PL23 1AH
Tel: 01726 832211 • Fax: 01726 832901
e-mail: hillandson@talk21.com
www.foweyharbourcottages.co.uk**

ETC ★★ – ★★★★

FREE AND REDUCED RATE HOLIDAY VISITS!

Don't miss our

Readers' Offer Vouchers

on pages 163-180

CHALETS • CARAVANS • CAMPING

St Ives Bay Holiday Park is set in sand dunes which run down to its own sandy beach. Many units have superb sea views. There is a large indoor pool and 2 clubs with FREE entertainment on the Park.

CALL OUR 24hr BROCHURE LINE

0800 317713

www.stivesbay.co.uk

CREEKSIDE HOLIDAY HOUSES

- Spacious houses, sleep 2/4/6/8.
- Peaceful, picturesque water's edge hamlet.
- Boating facilities
- Use of boat. • Own quay, beach.
- Secluded gardens • Near Pandora Inn.
- Friday bookings • Dogs welcome.

**PETER WATSON,
CREEKSIDE HOLIDAY HOUSES,
RESTRONGUET, FALMOUTH TR11 5ST
Tel: 01326 372722**

www.creeksideholidayhouses.co.uk

Penquite Farm
Golant, Fowey PL23 1LB

A stunning location in spectacular scenic countryside offering wonderful river views over the Fowey Valley. A perfect rural retreat for a relaxing, enjoyable holiday on a working farm, nestling beside a beautiful 13th century church on the edge of a peaceful riverside village.

A spacious, three-bedroom, split-level house with two bathrooms, and two beautifully restored barn conversions, all rooms en suite and tastefully furnished to a very high standard. Sleep four (wheelchair-friendly), six and ten persons. All have own large gardens, patio area, BBQs and ample parking. Ideal for touring, walking, beaches, National Trust properties, gardens, and the Eden Project close by.

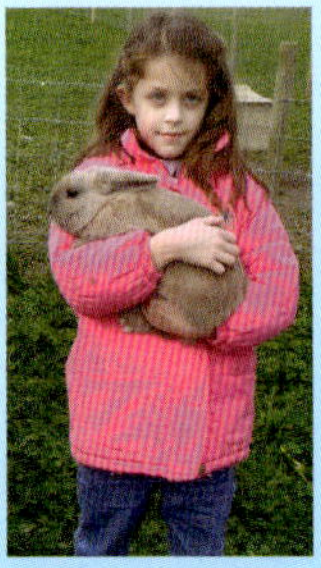

Ruth Varco • Tel & Fax: 01726 833319

ruth@penquitefarm.co.uk
www.penquitefarm.co.uk

Forget-Me-Not Farm Holidays

Situated on Trefranck, our 340-acre family-run beef and sheep farm, in North Cornwall, on the edge of enchanting Bodmin Moor and six miles from the spectacular North Cornwall Heritage Coast. We offer all year round luxury, 4-star, self-catering acccommodation.

◆ **Forget-Me-Not Cottage** can comfortably sleep 6 and is tastefully decorated and superbly equipped, with a real log fire and central heating.

◆ **The Old Wagon House** is a stylish barn conversion and sleeps 2-4, with a 4-poster bed – ideal for romantic breaks. Mobility rating.

◆ **The Stable** is an en suite twin annexe to the Old Wagon House.

◆ **Honeysuckle Cottage** sleeps 5. Lovely views of the moor; beautiful garden. Well equipped.

◆ **Meadowsweet Cottage** - barn conversion, sleeps 4, surrounded by own woodlands. Abundance of wildlife. Excellent for cycling and walking holidays.

Trefranck is within easy reach of the Eden Project, the Lost Gardens of Heligan, Padstow and the Camel Trail.

Visit Bude, Crackington Haven, Padstow, Boscastle, Tintagel & The Eden Project.

Trefranck Farm, St Clether, Launceston PL15 8QN
Mobile: 07790 453229
Tel: 01566 86284
e-mail: holidays@trefranck.co.uk
www.forget-me-not-farm-holidays.co.uk

Cornwall

Bamham Farm Cottages
Higher Bamham, Launceston PL15 9LD

Situated in beautiful countryside, the panoramic views from Higher Bamham across the Tamar valley to Dartmoor are superb. Our seven cottages were converted from the 18th century farmhouse and outbuildings and can accommodate between 4 and 8 people each or up to 41 for larger groups, celebrations and special occasions. The heated indoor swimming pool with dedicated paddling area (open all year) and games room (new for 2009) provide the perfect base for a family holiday. The farm is only one mile from Launceston town centre, historic capital of Cornwall with all local conveniences and providing easy access to North Coast beaches and coastal villages, South Coast beaches and fishing ports, Bodmin Moor, Dartmoor National Park and the Eden Project. Most of the nearest North Coast and South Coast beaches are dog friendly details of which are provided on arrival. Flexible Short Breaks are available year round except during school holidays. The cottages are all well equipped and have VisitBritain 4-star rating. A weekend in Cornwall has never been easier, we're only one mile from the A30 and 35 minutes from the M5.

Contact • Simon and Clare Hirsh • Tel: 01566 772141
e-mail:simon@bamhamfarm.co.uk • www.bamhamfarm.co.uk

CUTKIVE WOOD HOLIDAY LODGES

Nestling in the heart of a peaceful family-owned country estate are six well-equipped comfortable cedar-clad lodges. Set on the edge of ancient bluebell woods with lovely rural views, you can relax and enjoy yourself in this tranquil and idyllic setting. Help with the animals, explore the woods and fields, fun play area. So much for everyone to see and do – memorable beaches, wonderful coasts, walk the moors, inspiring gardens and Eden, theme attractions, historic gems. Dogs welcome. Ideally situated to enjoy coast and country holidays whatever the time of year.

St Ive, Liskeard, Cornwall PL14 3ND • Tel: 01579 362216
www.cutkivewood.co.uk • e-mail: holidays@cutkivewood.co.uk

Cornwall

A unique Cornish 4 star holiday experience

Set in 55 acres of rolling countryside well away from the road and with stunning views of Looe Island and the sea beyond Tregoad Park offers the ideal location for both fun filled family holidays and quiet relaxing out of season breaks. Close to the pretty fishing town of Looe and beaches we can guarantee you a beautiful location, all the facilities and a very warm and friendly welcome. We have 190 large flat & terraced pitches of which 60 are hardstanding ideal for touring caravans, motorhomes and tents. Most are southerly facing and all pitches have electric hook-up. There are ample water and waste points around the park and access roads are tarmac so getting on and off your pitch is easy. The toilet and shower facilities are modern, clean and free of charge and there is a launderette and disabled wet room at the upper block. The reception building contains a well stocked shop and visitor information centre together with internet access point and post box.

Tregoad Park, St Martin, Near Looe, Cornwall PL13 1PB • Tel: 01503 262718
Fax: 01503 264777 • e-mail: info@tregoadpark.co.uk • www.tregoadpark.co.uk

TREMAINE GREEN
for MEMORABLE HOLIDAYS

"A beautiful private hamlet" of 11 traditional cosy Cornish craftsmen's cottages between Looe and Polperro. Clean, comfortable and well equipped, with a warm friendly atmosphere, for 2 to 8 people. Set in award-winning grounds, only 12 miles from the Eden Project with country and coastal walks nearby. Rates from only £126. Pets welcome at £18 pw.

Towels, Linen, Electric & Hot Water included • Dishwashers in larger cottages
Launderette • Kid's Play Area • Games Room • Tennis Court • TV/DVDs • Wi-Fi
Cots & Highchairs • Pubs & Restaurants in walking distance • Activities Area

Mr & Mrs J Spreckley, Tremaine Green Country Cottages,
Pelynt, Near Looe, Cornwall PL13 2LT • Tel: 01503 220333
www.tremainegreen.co.uk
e-mail: stay@tremainegreen.co.uk

Cornwall

Trevarthian Holiday Homes • Marazion

High quality Victorian cottages and apartments in the prime Mount's Bay location. Superb views of St Michael's Mount, Mousehole, Newlyn, Penzance.
A selection of the finest self-catering accommodation available.
One minute walk to safe, sandy beach. Playground, pubs, restaurants, galleries, shops, bus routes for Land's End, St Ives, Penzance.
Sleep 1-5 • Low Season £170-£320 per week,
High Season £420-£830 per week • Open all year • NO SMOKING

Contact Mr Sean Cattran, Trevarthian Holiday Homes, West End, Marazion TR17 0EG
Tel: 01736 710100 • Fax: 01736 710111 • info@trevarthian.co.uk • www.trevarthian.co.uk

WATERGATE BAY TOURING PARK

HEATED OUTDOOR POOL
CAFETERIA · LAUNDERETTE
INDIVIDUAL PITCHES
NO OVERCROWDING
LEVEL SITE · ELECTRIC HOOKUPS
FULLY LICENSED CLUBHOUSE
AMUSEMENT ARCADE
KIDS PLAY AREA
SELF SERVICE SHOP
FREE EVENING ENTERTAINMENT
FREE COURTESY MINIBUS
TO THE BEACH
(DURING PEAK SEASON)

www.watergatebaytouringpark.co.uk
email@watergatebaytouringpark.co.uk

TELEPHONE
01637 860387
FAX
0871 661 7549

Please note

All the information in this book is given in good faith in the belief that it is correct. However, the publishers cannot guarantee the facts given in these pages, neither are they responsible for changes in policy, ownership or terms that may take place after the date of going to press. Readers should always satisfy themselves that the facilities they require are available and that the terms, if quoted, still apply.

Cornwall

Harlyn Sands HOLIDAY PARK

Family owned, family run for families

★ STRICTLY FAMILIES ONLY ★

Enjoy a good old family Bucket and Spade Holiday on this golden sandy beach. Miles of coastal walks and award-winning waters. Top class family entertainment*, immaculate luxurious accommodation.
Fish and Chippy, Arcade. Children's Play Park, Kids' Club mornings, afternoons and evenings.
On-site Shop, Launderette, Shower Block, Electric Hook-Ups.

SUPER SPLASH FUN POOL
with toddlers' pool, flume and rapids**

Situated right on Trevose Head, 3 miles from Padstow, 12 miles from Newquay, only 30 minutes from the Eden Project.

Lighthouse Road, Trevose Head, Padstow, Cornwall PL28 8SQ
e-mail: harlyn@freenet.co.uk
www.harlynsands.co.uk

RING OUR BROCHURE HOTLINE:
01841 520720

*main season; during quiet times limited services available.** small charges apply; restrictions apply for non-swimmers.

Self-Catering Accommodation, St Ives Bay, Cornwall

sandbank holidays
ST IVES BAY

High quality Apartments and Bungalows for 2-6 persons. Peaceful garden setting close to miles of sandy beach, acres of grassy dunes and SW Coastal Path. Fully equipped for your self-catering holiday. Heated, colour TV, microwave etc. Spotlessly clean. Children's play area. Dogs Welcome.

All major debit and credit cards accepted.

Sandbank Holidays
51 Upton Towans, Hayle, Cornwall TR27 5BL
Tel: 01736 752594
www.sandbank-holidays.co.uk

Cornwall

Children and pet-friendly

Whitsand Bay Self Catering Holidays have Holiday Houses, Cottages and Villas, sleeping 4-10, to rent in Portwrinkle in Cornwall. Portwrinkle itself is located directly on the UK's heritage coastline in a designated Area of Outstanding Natural Beauty. All our accommodation has sea views and is priced to suit all pockets. Whatever your holiday requirements, we're sure you'll find something to your liking, be it an active holiday with golf, swimming, walking or fishing, or just relaxing on our local beaches. For those more culturally minded there are historic fishing villages, historic homes and gardens as well as the Eden Project and Lost Gardens of Heligan, both only 40 minutes away.

Tel: 01579 345688
e-mail: ehwbsc@hotmail.com

CHAPEL COTTAGES   ST TUDY

Four traditional cottages, sleeping 2 to 5, in a quiet farming area. Ideal for the spectacular north coast, Bodmin Moor, and the Eden Project. Comfortable and well-equipped. Garden and private parking. Rental £175 to £475 per week. Also two cottages for couples at Hockadays, near Blisland - converted from a 17th century barn in a quiet farming hamlet. Rental £175 to £360 per week. Shop and pub/ restaurant within walking distance. Regretfully, no pets. Brochure available.

Mrs M. Pestell, 'Hockadays', Tregenna, Blisland PL30 4QJ • Tel: 01208 850146
www.hockadays.co.uk

Summer Valley Touring Park
Shortlanesend, Truro TR4 9DW

Situated just two miles from Truro, Cornwall's cathedral city, and ideally placed as a centre for touring all parts of Cornwall. This quiet, small, secluded site is only one-and-a-half miles from the main A30 and its central situation is advantageous for North Cornwall's beautiful surfing beaches and rugged Atlantic coast or Falmouth's quieter and placid fishing coves. Horse riding, fishing and golf are all available within easy distance. This compact site is personally supervised by the owners. Facilities include a toilet block with free hot water, washing cubicles, showers, shaving points, launderette, iron, hairdryer, etc; caravan electric hook-ups; children's play area. Shop with dairy products, groceries, bread, confectionery, toys, Calor/Camping gas.

Mr and Mrs C.R. Simpkins • Tel: 01872 277878 • www.summervalley.co.uk

Two people, car, caravan/tent £12 to £15 per day

SOUTH DEVON

Best Beaches

As Britain's prime holiday area it is not surprising that South Devon is rich in fine beaches. Quality Coast Awards went to several beaches around this delightful coastline, where standards of cleanliness, safety and environmental management satisfied strict criteria.

 South West Tourism
(Bristol & Bath, Cornwall, Devon, Dorset, Gloucestershire & The Cotswolds, Somerset, Wiltshire).

- Tel: 0870 442 0880
- Fax: 0870 442 0881
- e-mail: info@swtourism.org.uk
- www.visitsouthwest.co.uk

BLUE FLAG BEACHES 2009
- *Dawlish Warren*
- *Blackpool Sands*
- *Challaborough*
- *Bigbury-on-Sea*
- *Torbay*
  Breakwater
  Meadfoot
  Oddicombe
  Broadsands

Woodlands Leisure Park Dartmouth

For more information about holidaying in South Devon see:
- www.visitsouthdevon.co.uk
  www.englishriviera.co.uk
- www.southdevonaonb.org.uk

South Devon

EXMOUTH

Family Fun Activities: Indoor swimming pool, children's playground, boating lake, indoor sports centre, amusement arcade, mini-railway • Bowls, tennis, indoor tennis centre, putting, cricket, approach golf • Boat trips, angling • Old tyme and modern dancing,

Special Events: End July: Carnival events. **October:** Winter Floodlit Carnival.

Tourist Information Centre,
Alexandra Terrace, Exmouth EX8 INZ
Tel: 01395 222299
e-mail: info@exmouthtourism.co.uk
www.exmouthguide.co.uk

Beaches

• MAER, RODNEY BAY AND EXMOUTH BEACH. Beaches two-and-a-half miles long. Rodney Bay naturally sheltered, others open; promenade and good parking. *Safety and maintenance:* warning flags, lifeguards peak summer season; cleaned daily. *Beach facilities:* deck chairs, swings; beach huts for hire from T.I.C.; ice-cream kiosks, snack bars, restaurants and pubs; toilets with access. *Dog restrictions:* banned from main beach from 1st May to 30th September.

PLYMOUTH

Family Fun Activities: Plymouth Pavilions with leisure pool, ice-skating, bar, bistro and shops • Mayflower Visitor Centre • National Marine Aquarium • Sports centre, indoor and outdoor swimming pools, parks with children's playgrounds • Tennis, putting, bowls, squash, dry-ski slope, bowling • Marina and water sports centre, sailing schools, sea angling • Theatre, multi-screen cinemas; museum and art gallery.

Special Events: May: Lord Mayor's Day; Vehicle and Bus Rally. **June:** Plymouth Playfair. **July:** Saltram Fair. **July:** Half Marathon. **August:** National Fireworks Championships. **September:** Heritage Open Days. **November:** Christmas Lights.

Tourist Information Centre, Plymouth Mayflower, The Barbican, Plymouth
Tel: 01752 306330
e-mail: barbicantic@plymouth.gov.uk
www.plymouth.gov.uk

Beaches

• BEACHES. The city itself has an attractive waterfront with sheltered promenades and rock pools, and a fully restored Art Deco Lido. There are good parking facilities, toilets, ice-cream kiosks, snack bars, and family restaurants/pubs.

SIDMOUTH

Family Fun Activities: Children's playgrounds • Cricket, golf, angling, sailing, putting, tennis, bowls.

Special Events: August: International Folk Festival. **September:** Sidmouth Carnival.

Tourist Information Centre,
Ham Lane, Sidmouth • 01395 516441
e-mail: enquiries@sidmouth.co.uk
www.visitsidmouth.co.uk

Beaches

• MAIN BEACH. Half-a-mile long, shingle and sand at low tide; promenade and ample parking. *Safety and maintenance:* lifeguards present only on Sundays; cleaned daily. *Beach facilities:* beach huts, deck chairs; ice-cream kiosk; toilets with access. *Dog restrictions:* banned from 1st May to 30th September.

TEIGNMOUTH & SHALDON

Family Fun Activities: Victorian Pier • Children's play area • Outdoor heated pool • Crazy golf • Bowls • Angling • Golf course • Summer shows.

☆ **Special Events: June:** Folk Festival. **July/August:** Summer Fun Fest. **July:** Carnival and Regatta. **August:** Water Carnival and Regatta. **November:** Jazz Festival, Winter Carnival.

i Tourist Information Centre, The Den, Teignmouth TQ14 8BE • 01626 215666
e-mail: teigntic@teignbridge.gov.uk
www.southdevon.org.uk

Beaches

• **TEIGNMOUTH TOWN BEACH.** Long, sandy beach stretching from mouth of River Teign east towards Dawlish. *Safety and maintenance:* information signage, lifeguard patrol May-Sept; lifesaving equipment; daily beach cleaning. *Beach facilities:* deck chairs; beach wheelchair for hire; ice-cream kiosks and snack bars; toilets, showers; (& access to beach). *Dog restrictions:* not allowed on designated areas of the beach from 1st May to 30th Sept.

• **NESS BEACH, SHALDON.** Shingle beach sloping gently to the sea; safe bathing, rock pools at low tide No & access. *Safety and maintenance:* lifesaving equipment, information signage; daily beach cleaning. *Beach facilities:* shops and toilets nearby. *Dog restrictions:* none.

FREE AND REDUCED RATE HOLIDAY VISITS!
Don't miss our
Readers' Offer Vouchers
on pages 163-180

DAWLISH

Family Fun Activities: Sports centre •Amusement arcades • Approach golf, putting, crazy golf, bowls • Angling • Theatre • Boat trips •Visitor Centre at Dawlish Warren Nature Reserve.

☆ **Special Events: June:** Arts Festival. **July/August:** Summer Fun Fest. **August:** Carnival.

i Tourist Information Centre, The Lawn, Dawlish EX7 9PW • 01626 215665
e-mail: dawtic@teignbridge.gov.uk
www.southdevon.org.uk

Beaches

• **DAWLISH TOWN BEACH.** Mixture of sand and shingle, gently sloping to sea; safe family beach a short walk from town centre; poor & access. *Safety and maintenance:* information signage, lifesaving equipment; cleaned daily. *Beach facilities:* deck chairs, ice-cream kiosks and snack bars; toilets with & access. *Dog restrictions:* not allowed on designated areas of the beach from 1st May to 30th September.

• **CORYTON COVE.** Secluded, sandy beach within easy walking distance of town centre; & access. *Safety and maintenance:* information signage, lifesaving equipment; cleaned daily. *Beach facilities:* beach hut hire, snack bar; toilets with & access, showers. *Dog restrictions:* not allowed on designated areas of the beach from 1st May to 30th September.

• **DAWLISH WARREN.** Golden sands backed by sand dunes; easy access from main roads, good public transport links; & access. *Safety and maintenance:* information signage, lifeguards May to September, lifeasaving equipment; cleaned daily. *Beach facilities:* deck chairs; ice-cream kiosks and snack bars; toilets with & access, showers. *Dog restrictions:* not allowed from slipway to groyne from 1st April to 30th September.

TORQUAY

Family Fun Activities: Windsurfing, sailing, angling • Indoor pools • Crazy golf, putting, tennis, squash, ten-pin bowling • Cinema, theatres, nightclubs, casino • Riviera Leisure Centre, museum, Babbacombe Model Village, cliff railway, Living Coasts.

☆ **Special Events:** **August:** Torbay Royal Regatta.

[i] The Tourist Information Centre, Vaughan Parade, Torquay TQ2 5JG
Tel: 01803 211211
e-mail: holiday@torbay.gov.uk
www.englishriviera.co.uk

Beaches

- **TORRE ABBEY SANDS.** 600 yards long, sandy and naturally sheltered; easy access, ample parking nearby. *Safety and maintenance:* warning flags, lifesaving equipment. *Beach facilities:* cafe/ refreshments; toilets nearby. *Dog restrictions:* dogs banned.
- **ANSTEY'S COVE.** 220 yards long, rock and shingle. Access steep in places. Parking 10 minutes' walk. *Safety and maintenance:* warning flags, lifesaving equipment. *Beach facilities:* refreshments, beach shop; toilets nearby. *Dog restrictions:* dogs allowed.
- **MEADFOOT BEACH.** 350 yards long, pebble and sand; easy access and ample parking. *Safety and maintenance:* lifesaving equipment. Lost Child centre. *Beach facilities:* cafe/ refreshments; toilets with baby changing facilities. *Dog restrictions:* allowed (Kilmorlie end).
- **ODDICOMBE BEACH.** 400 yards long, sand and shingle; access via clifflift. Parking 15 minutes' walk. *Safety and maintenance:* warning flags, lifesaving equipment, first aid post. *Beach facilities:* deck chair/sunbed hire; beach cafe/refreshments, beach shop; toilets with access and baby changing facilities. *Dog restrictions:* banned.

PAIGNTON

Family Fun Activities: Pier • Quay West water park and beach resort • Steam railway, amusement arcade, zoo, leisure centre with swimming pool • Boat trips, angling • Squash, badminton, tennis, putting, golf, go karting • Multiplex cinema, theatre.

☆ **Special Events:** **July:** Torbay Carnival. **August:** Paignton Regatta, Children's Festival.

[i] Paignton TIC, Esplanade Road, Paignton TQ4 6ED • Tel: 01803 211211
e-mail: holiday@torbay.gov.uk
www.englishriviera.co.uk

Beaches

- **BROADSANDS BEACH.** Sandy beach, one-and-a-half miles long; easy access and ample parking. *Safety and maintenance:* warning flags, life-saving equipment, first aid post. *Beach facilities:* deck chair/chalet hire; refreshments, beach shop; toilets with access. *Dog restrictions:* banned.
- **GOODRINGTON SANDS.** 1200 yards long, sandy; ample parking. *Safety and maintenance:* warning flags. Lost Child centre. Patrol boat in operation. *Beach facilities:* deck chair/sunbed hire; cafe/ refreshments and restaurant, beach shop; toilets with access. *Dog restrictions:* banned on South Sands, allowed on North Sands.
- **PAIGNTON SANDS.** Sandy with rock pools, 1200 yards long; promenade and pier with arcades. *Safety and maintenance:* warning flags, life-saving equipment, first aid post. Lost Child centre. *Beach facilities:* deck chair/ sunbed hire; cafe/refreshments, restaurant, beach shop; toilets with access. *Dog restrictions:* banned.
- **PRESTON SANDS.** 600 yards long, sandy and naturally sheltered. *Safety and maintenance:* warning flags, life-saving equipment. *Beach facilities:* deck chair/ sunbed/chalet hire; cafe/refreshments, beach shop; toilets (toilets with access nearby). *Dog restrictions:* banned.

BRIXHAM

Family Fun Activities: Indoor and outdoor swimming pools • Tennis, squash, mini-golf, putting, leisure centre • Fishing trips/cruises, sailing • Berry Head Country Park • Golden Hind replica, museums.

Special Events: May: Heritage Festival. **June:** Brixham Trawler Race. **July:** Brixham Happnin!!. **August:** Brixham Regatta.

Brixham T.I.C., Old Market House, The Quay, Brixham TQ5 8AW
Tel: 01803 211211
e-mail: holiday@torbay.gov.uk
www.englishriviera.co.uk

Beaches

- **BREAKWATER BEACH.** Shingle beach, 100 yards long; easy access and ample parking; access difficult. *Safety and maintenance:* warning flags, life-saving equipment. *Beach facilities:* deck chairs; cafe/refreshments and restaurant; toilets. *Dog restrictions:* banned.

- **SHOALSTONE BEACH.** Shingle, with rock pools and sea water swimming pool; access difficult. *Safety and maintenance:* warning flags, lifeguards, life-saving equipment. *Beach facilities:* deck chair/sunbed hire; cafe; toilets with baby changing facilities. *Dog restrictions:* banned from sea water swimming pool

- **ST MARY'S BAY.** Sand and shingle, parking 10 minutes' walk; access difficult. *Safety and maintenance:* swimming safe with care. *Dog restrictions:* allowed.

☆ Fun for all the Family ☆

◆ **Babbacombe Model Village (01803 315315).** Masterpiece of miniature landscaping - hundreds of models and figures.
www.babbacombemodelvillage.co.uk

◆ **Dartmoor Zoological Park, Sparkwell (01752 837645).** Over 200 animals ranging from tigers, bears and wolves to birds of prey and even guinea pigs.
www.dartmoorzoologicalpark.co.uk

◆ **Kent's Cavern Show Caves, Torquay (01803 215136).** Stalactite caves of great beauty. Guided tours to discover the magic of Britain's earliest known settlement.
www.kents-cavern.co.uk

◆ **National Marine Aquarium, Plymouth (01752 600301).** New attraction where memorable sights include a wall of ocean 15 metres wide and a shark theatre in over 700,000 litres of water.
www.national-aquarium.co.uk

◆ **Pennywell Farm & Wildlife Centre, Buckfastleigh (01364 642023).** A unique Devon family day out with hands-on activities and crafts. Ponies and piglets, quad bikes and train rides - there's always something going on.
www.pennywellfarmcentre.co.uk

South Devon

Standing in four acres of mature subtropical gardens, overlooking two miles of sandy beach, yet within easy reach of Dartmoor and Exeter, Devoncourt provides an ideal base for a family holiday.

BEDROOMS: The accommodation is in 52 single, double or family rooms, all with private bathroom, colour TV, tea and coffee making facilities and telephone.

LEISURE: Swimming pool, sauna, steam room, whirlpool spa, solarium and fitness centre, snooker room, hair and beauty salon. For those who prefer to be out of doors there is a tennis court, croquet lawn, attractive outdoor heated pool, 18 hole putting green and golf practice area, all within the grounds.

DINING: Attractive lounge bar and restaurant overlooking the fabulous gardens, with fantastic sea views from the large picture windows. Children's menus and vegetarian options available.

DEVONCOURT Douglas Avenue, Exmouth, Devon EX8 2EX
Tel: 01395 272277 • Fax: 01395 269315
e-mail: enquiries@devoncourt.com • www.devoncourthotel.com

South Devon

BURTON FARMHOUSE Galmpton, Kingsbridge TQ7 3EY • Tel: 01548 561210
Fax: 01548 562257 • e-mail: anne@burtonfarm.co.uk • www.burtonfarmhouse.co.uk

Anne Rossiter welcomes you to Burton Farmhouse, a charming and relaxing place to stay in an area of outstanding natural beauty in the South Hams. There is a choice of 14 pretty en suite rooms, centrally heated, with tea/coffee making facilities. Stay in one of our self-catering cottages here in the heart of the lovely South Hams of South Devon. Our pretty cottages are located close to Burton Farmhouse where guests can use the Garden Room Restaurant for hearty, farmhouse breakfasts, evening dinners, Sunday lunches and afternoon cream teas. The Garden Room Restaurant uses fresh, seasonal, local produce to create tasty traditional home cooked farmhouse fayre in a friendly and relaxed atmosphere.

BURTON FARMHOUSE

Bovey Castle is a family friendly hotel, offering luxury holiday accommodation in Devon for parents with children of all ages. This wonderful sporting estate is like a huge playground, with activities designed to give everyone a great time out in the beautiful Devon countryside.

Parents can relax while their young children are well looked after by qualified staff at *The Playroom*, which has exciting games and creative activities planned every day.

We welcome the tiniest guests and all facilities needed for baby care are available. Babysitting services can be arranged in advance, to ensure parents can enjoy a relaxed evening during their stay.

Family Rooms: these open plan rooms are large enough to accommodate 2 children up to the age of 16 on a sofa bed or extra bed. All of the rooms are individually decorated to a high standard and have a small seating area.

Bovey Castle

North Bovey
Dartmoor National Park
Devon TQ13 8RE
Tel: 01647 445000
Fax: 01647 445020
enquiries@boveycastle.com
www.boveycastle.com

South Devon

your family memories await...

An inspiring collection of holiday cottages throughout the West Country. Our stunning rural and coastal locations are perfect for you and your little ones

holidaycottages.co.uk
01237 459897

Cornwall | Devon | Somerset | Dorset

Lilac Cottage

Contact: **Mrs J. M. Stuart,
2 Sandford House, Kingsclere,
Newbury, Berkshire RG20 4PA**
Tel & Fax: **01635 291942**
Mobile: **07787 550413**
e-mail: **joanna.sb@free.fr**

Detached cottage, carefully renovated, retaining the inglenook fireplace, oak beams, floors and doors. Oil-fired central heating, colour TV, fully-equipped all-electric kitchen. Furnished to a high standard, sleeps six plus cot. Children and pets are welcome. Walled garden and garage. The villages and surrounding countryside are beautiful on the borders of Devon, Dorset, and Somerset. Many seaside towns within 10 miles – Lyme Regis, Charmouth and Seaton.

Smallridge, Axminster, Devon

South Devon   39

DEVONCOURT HOLIDAY FLATS

BERRYHEAD ROAD, BRIXHAM, DEVON TQ5 9AB

Devoncourt is a development of 24 self-contained flats, occupying one of the finest positions in Torbay, with unsurpassed views. At night the lights of Torbay are like a fairyland to be enjoyed from your very own balcony.

MasterCard VISA

EACH FLAT HAS:
Heating
Sea Views over Torbay
Private balcony
Own front door
Separate bathroom and toilet
Separate bedroom
Bed-settee in lounge
Lounge sea views over Marina
Kitchenette - all electric
Private car park
Opposite beach
Colour television
Overlooks lifeboat
Short walk to town centre
Double glazing
Open all year
Mini Breaks October to April

Tel: 01803 853748
(or 07802 403289 after office hours)
www.devoncourt.info

Woodlands
TOURING CARAVAN & CAMPING PARK
DARTMOUTH

AA Campsite of the Year

Best in Europe Award — Alan Rogers — Best Family Campsite

BEAUTIFUL RELAXED PARK

- Award Winning Facilities
- Spacious Pitches
- Licensed Shop
- Bath & Shower Rooms
- Superb setting & views
- Games & TV Room
- Opposite 27 hole Golf Course
- Adults midweek special

FREE ENTRY TO THEME PARK
when staying 2nts or more

STRETCH YOUR POUND FURTHER!

Woodlands Leisure Park, Blackawton, Totnes, South Devon TQ9 7DQ
Tel: 01803 712598 • www.woodlandspark.com
Woodlands Leisure reserve the right to close the park or any attractions without prior notice.

Regional Tourist Board MEMBER   AA

South Devon

West Banbury Farm Cottages...where relaxation is a way of life

Come to West Banbury and you'll discover a rural haven where you can unwind and relax. We are near Broadwoodwidger, West Devon, ideally located for exploring Devon and Cornwall, including the north and south coasts. Plenty of family attractions are within easy reach. We have ten charming cottages, each spacious and very comfortable, set around two courtyards with stunning views to Dartmoor. The cottages sleep 2 to 8. Large indoor heated pool, sauna, games room, children's play area, fun pitch and putt, and a grass tennis court. Open all year. Dogs welcome. Short breaks available.

For more information call Anna-Rose on 01566 780423

www.westbanbury.co.uk

Pennymoor
Caravan & Camping Park
Modbury, Devon PL21 0SB

Welcome to the leisurely, relaxed atmosphere of Pennymoor, a delightful and spacious rural camping and caravanning site with panoramic views of Dartmoor and Devon countryside...

Immaculately maintained, well-drained, peaceful rural site with panoramic views. Midway between Plymouth and Kingsbridge (A379). An ideal centre for touring moors, towns and beaches, only five miles from Bigbury-on-Sea and nine miles from Salcombe. Golf courses at Bigbury and Thurlestone and boating at Salcombe, Newton Ferrers and Kingsbridge. Large, superb toilet/shower block with fully tiled walls and floors, and hairdryers. Facilities for the disabled holidaymaker. Dishwashing room - FREE hot water. Laundry room. Children's play area. Shop. Gas. Public telephone on site. Luxury caravans for hire, all services, fully equipped including colour TV. Ideal for touring caravans and tents.

Write, phone or e-mail quoting FHG for free colour brochure.

Tel & Fax: 01548 830542 • Tel: 01548 830020
e-mail: enquiries@pennymoor-camping.co.uk
www.pennymoor-camping.co.uk

Sailing off the coast at Torquay

South Devon 41

Adventure Cottages

Tel: 01548 821784

it's all about family fun...

At Adventure Cottages it's all about family! Five beautifully appointed self catering cottages designed specifically for a family break or gathering - whatever the weather.

The perfect location for exploring the beautiful rugged South Devon coastline. Acres of rolling countryside to explore by foot or bicycle straight from your front door. Secure parking and storage of bikes and your leisure equipment.

On-site Adventure & Leisure Facilities
★ Soundproof Indoor Off-Road arena - Juniors (7yrs+) to adults. First Junior lesson free with week-long booking
★ Indoor swimming pool with private changing rooms and showers
★ Games room with full sized American pool table, table tennis table, table football, video library, infants and toddlers' toys
★ Enclosed playing field with trampoline and zip wire

Cottage Facilities
The five beautifully renovated traditional stone cottages are totally self contained with all the modern amenities that you will need for the perfect family break.
★ Cottages sleep 4-10 people (+ cots)
★ Dog friendly
★ BBQ
★ Crackling wood burners
★ Flexible living accommodation
★ Fully equipped kitchen including; cooker, fridge/freezer, dishwasher, microwave
★ Colour television with DVD/VHS player in all cottages
★ En-suite bathrooms to master bedrooms
★ Free WiFi Access available
★ Cots, highchairs, stair-gates included for children

Activities in the surrounding Area:
★ Ideally placed to explore South Devon, minutes from A38
★ Woodlands Leisure Park - 10 minutes
★ Horse riding, Golf, Watersports - all on your doorstep
★ Close to Dartmouth, Totnes, and the Dartmoor National Park

Open 365 days a year, Adventure Cottages is the perfect location to unwind from the stress of modern day life... Short breaks also available

www.adventurecottages.co.uk
01548 821784
info@adventurecottages.co.uk
Instant online booking facility

South Devon

A quiet, family-run park with 68 modern and luxury caravans for hire. The park overlooks the delightful River Axe Valley, and is just a 10 minute walk from the town with its wonderfully long, award-winning beach. Children will love our extensive play area, with its sand pit, paddling pool, swings and slide. Laundry facilities are provided and there is a wide selection of goods on sale in the park shop which is open every day. All of our caravans have a shower, toilet, fridge, and TV with digital channels. Also, with no clubhouse, a relaxing atmosphere is ensured. Prices from £80 per week; reductions for three or fewer persons early/late season.

Axevale Caravan Park
Colyford Road, Seaton, Devon EX12 2DF
Tel: 0800 0688816
e-mail: info@axevale.co.uk
www.axevale.co.uk

☆ Fun for all the Family ☆

◆ **Pennywell Farm & Wildlife Centre, Buckfastleigh (01364 642023).** A unique Devon family day out with hands-on activities and crafts. Ponies and piglets, quad bikes and train rides - there's always something going on.
www.pennywellfarmcentre.co.uk

◆ **Paignton Zoo (01803 697500).** Over 300 species in spacious landscaped enclosures. Miniature railway, restaurant, activity centre.
www.paigntonzoo.org.uk

◆ **Paignton and Dartmouth Steam Railway (01803 555872).** Seven-mile trip along the spectacular Torbay coast; gift shop, buffet.
www.paignton-steamrailway.co.uk

◆ **River Dart Country Park, Ashburton (01364 652511).** Country fun for everyone - children's adventure playgrounds, nature trails, picnic meadow. Can be combined with river cruise.
www.riverdart.co.uk

◆ **South Devon Railway, Buckfastleigh (0845 345 1420).** Excursion trips on steam trains; museum, picnic area and play area.
www.southdevonrailway.org

◆ **Woodlands Leisure Park, Dartmouth (01803 712598).** Lots of family fun activities, indoor and outdoor, plus hundreds of animals and birds.
www.woodlands-leisure-park.co.uk

Mark and Judy Harrison welcome you to

THE ROYAL OAK INN
Dunsford, Devon

The Royal Oak is a traditional village pub with a friendly atmosphere, a large Beer Garden, and beautiful views across Dunsford and the Teign Valley. Quiet, newly refurbished en suite bedrooms are available in the tastefully converted 400 year old granite and cob barn located to the rear of the Inn. All non-smoking. Each room has its own front door which opens out onto a pretty, walled courtyard. Ideal base for touring Dartmoor, Exeter and the coast. Great for children, with our own play area and lots of animals. Dogs on leads are welcome. Plenty of off-road parking.

The Royal Oak Inn
Dunsford, Near Exeter, Devon EX6 7DA
TEL: 01647 252256 • e-mail: mark@troid.co.uk • www.royaloakd.com

Strathmore

A delightful family-friendly licensed Victorian guest house, situated just a 10-minute stroll to both the town centre and seafront. With 8 individually designed en suite bedrooms, cosy lounge bar, secluded terraced gardens and parking. Children of all ages welcome, cots and high chairs available. Small well-behaved dogs over 18 months old also welcome.

Contacts: either Pete or Heather Small

57 St Brannocks Road
Ilfracombe EX34 8EQ
Tel: 01271 862248
e-mail: info@the-strathmore.co.uk
www.the-strathmore.co.uk

North Devon

- **TUNNELS BEACHES.** 600 yards long, shingle with rock pools and cliffs; naturally sheltered, good parking. *Safety and maintenance:* warning signs, certain parts cut off at high tide; beach privately owned and cleaned daily during season. *Beach facilities:* deck chairs, sports canoes, rowing boats; ice-cream kiosk and snack bar; toilets, cafe, children's indoor play area.

- **WHITE PEBBLE BEACH.** 220 yards long, shingle and pebbles. Cliffs, naturally sheltered; parking. *Safety and maintenance:* warning signs, certain parts cut off at high tide.

- **WILDERSMOUTH BEACH.** 220 yards long, shingle with rock pools; naturally sheltered; promenade, good parking. *Safety and maintenance:* cleaned by Local Authority. *Beach facilities:* ice-cream kiosks, snack bars, restaurants and pubs; ramps with ♿ access.

BRITAIN'S BEST BEACHES
See pages 8-11

WOOLACOMBE

Family Fun Activities: Repertory theatre and other entertainment in season.

⭐ **Special Events: July:** Grand Sandcastle Competition. **September:** National Surf Life Saving Championships (every 3rd year). Other surf and water competitions during year.

ℹ️ Tourist Information Centre, The Esplanade, Woolacombe EX34 7DL • 01271 870553
e-mail: info@woolacombetourism.co.uk
www.woolacombetourism.co.uk

Beaches

WOOLACOMBE SANDS BEACH. 3 miles long, sandy and naturally sheltered; good parking. *Safety and maintenance:* flagged, warning signs, lifeguards (May to September); cleaned daily. *Beach facilities* (May to September): deck chairs, beach huts, children's amusements, ice-cream kiosks, snack bars, restaurants and pubs; toilets with ♿ access. *Dog restrictions:* some restricted areas in operation May to September. Blue Flag and Seaside Award since 1991. England for Excellence Award for Best Family Holiday 1999.

⭐ Fun for all the Family ⭐

◆ **Arlington Court (NT), Barnstaple (01271 850296).** A fascinating collection including a large collection of horse-drawn carriages. Surrounding park has a flock of Jacob's sheep, red deer and peacocks.
www.nationaltrust.org.uk

◆ **The Big Sheep, Abbotsham (01237 472366).** All you ever wanted to know about sheep – lots of lambs, plus sheep dairy, shearing, sheepdog trials. Ewetopia indoor playground. Shop and restaurant.
www.thebigsheep.co.uk

◆ **Gnome Reserve, Near Bradworthy (01409 241435).** For the young at heart - from 1 to 101! Four acres of woodland, meadow and garden is home to over 1000 gnomes and pixies. Gnome hats loaned free of charge to make you feel at home!
www.gnomereserve.co.uk

◆ **Combe Martin Wildlife and Dinosaur Park (01271 882486).** Otters, falcons, nature walks, children's playground and zoo, large indoor model railway.
www.dinosaur-park.com

North Devon

LYNTON & LYNMOUTH

Family Fun Activities: Children's playgrounds • Putting, tennis, bowls, cricket, horse riding • Boat trips, river and sea fishing • Cinema • Brass rubbing, museum • Local crafts centre • Unique water-operated cliff railway linking twin resorts.

Tourist Information Centre, Town Hall, Lynton
0845 660 3232 • Fax: 01598 752755
e-mail: info@lyntourism.co.uk
www.lyntourism.co.uk

Beaches

• **LEE BAY BEACH.** Half-a-mile long, sand and shingle, with access through Valley of Rocks and on to Lee Abbey bottom lodge (toll charge); parking in field overlooking sea. *Safety and maintenance:* safe within the bay, cleaned whenever necessary. *Beach facilities:* refreshments five minutes' walk (restricted opening), toilets two minutes' walk. *Dog restrictions:* banned.

• **LYNMOUTH BEACH.** Large rocky beach, long slipway, Rhenish tower guarding harbour. *Safety and maintenance:* safe within the bay, cleaned whenever necessary. *Dog restrictions:* none.

Fun on the roller coaster at The Milky Way Adventure Park, Clovelly

ILFRACOMBE

Family Fun Activities: Heated indoor pool, children's playground • Pier, angling • Tennis, putting, pitch and putt, crazy golf, golf course • Theatre, cinema, discos.

Tourist Information Centre, The Seafront, Ilfracombe EX34 9BZ
01271 863001
e-mail: info@vistilfracombe.co.uk
www.vistilfracombe.co.uk

☆ **Special Events: June:** Victorian Celebration. **July:** North Devon Arts Youth Festival. **August:** Emergency Rescue Service Display. **August/September:** Flower Shows.

Beaches

• **HARBOUR BEACH.** 200 yards long, sandy and naturally sheltered; good parking. Promenade, pier with arcade and cafe; toilets and parking. *Beach facilities:* ice-cream kiosks, snack bars, restaurants and pubs; toilets with ♿ access.

• **HELE BAY BEACH.** Half-a-mile long, shingle (some sand) with rock pools; promenade, good parking. *Safety and maintenance:* cleaned regularly during season. *Beach facilities:* ice-cream kiosk, snack bars, restaurants and pubs; toilets with ♿ access

• **LARKSTONE BEACH.** 100 yards long, shingle and rock pools, naturally sheltered; good parking. *Safety and maintenance:* cleaned regularly in season. *Beach facilities:* ice-cream kiosk; toilets with ♿ access.

• **RAPPAREE BEACH.** 220 yards long, shingle with rock pools and cliffs, naturally sheltered; promenade, good parking. *Safety and maintenance:* warning signs; certain parts cut off at high tide; cleaned regularly during season.

North Devon 43

NORTH DEVON

Best Beaches

Along with two other fine beaches from the area, Woolacombe Beach is once again a proud winner of a European Blue Flag, indicating strict beach management and the highest standard of bathing water under EC legislation. Quality Coast Awards also went to beaches in this area.

BLUE FLAG BEACHES 2009
- *Ilfracombe (Tunnels)*
- *Westward Ho!*
- *Woolacombe*

i South West Tourism
(Bristol & Bath, Cornwall, Devon, Dorset, Gloucestershire & The Cotswolds, Somerset, Wiltshire).

- **Tel: 0870 442 0880**
- **Fax: 0870 442 0881**
- **e-mail: info@swtourism.org.uk**
- **www.visitsouthwest.co.uk**

The Big Sheep, Abbotsham

For more information about holidaying in North Devon see:
- www.northdevon.com •
- www.visit-exmoor.co.uk
- www.northdevon-aonb.org.uk

North Devon

47

Situated on the South West Coastal Path with wonderful views, and delicious home cooking, the North Cliff is an ideal base for discovering Exmoor and the North Devon Coast. We welcome pets, children and groups.

Tel: 01598 752357
e-mail: holidays@northcliffhotel.co.uk
www.northcliffhotel.co.uk

The North Cliff Hotel
North Walk, Lynton,
North Devon EX35 6HJ

FOSFELLE COUNTRY HOUSE HOTEL
Hartland, Bideford, Devon EX39 6EF

This 17th century manor house is set in six acres of grounds in peaceful surroundings with large ornamental gardens and lawns. Fosfelle offers a friendly atmosphere with excellent food, a licensed bar, and a television lounge with log fires on chilly evenings; central heating throughout. There is a games room for children. The comfortable bedrooms, some en suite, all have washbasins and tea making facilities; family rooms and cots are available. Within easy reach of local beaches and ideal for touring Devon and Cornwall. Trout and coarse fishing, clay shooting available at the hotel; riding and golf nearby. Open all year. Reductions for children.

Telephone: 01237 441273

Partridge Arms Farm
Yeo Mill, West Anstey, South Molton, North Devon EX36 3NU

Now a working farm of over 200 acres, four miles west of Dulverton, "Partridge Arms Farm" was once a coaching inn and has been in the same family since 1906. Genuine hospitality and traditional farmhouse fare await you. Comfortable accommodation in double, twin and single rooms, some of which have en suite facilities. There is also an original four-poster bedroom. Children welcome.

Animals by arrangement • Residential licence • Open all year • Fishing and riding available nearby
FARM HOLIDAY GUIDE DIPLOMA WINNER • Bed and Breakfast from £28 • Evening Meal from £16.

Times gone by...For those who want to enjoy a break in more unusual circumstances, Partridge Arms Farm has a converted, self-catering railway carriage. The carriage is situated on the old Taunton to Barnstaple railway line and, as well as being fully equipped, it sleeps up to 6 people. Children are welcome to stay in the carriage, as are dogs. The railway line offers a delightful and fascinating walk. Visitors can also explore at their leisure the 200 acres of surrounding farmland, which is situated in the Southern foothills of Exmoor.
Prices start from £490 per week (no hidden extras). Daily rates available.

For further information contact Hazel Milton
Tel: 01398 341217
Fax: 01398 341569
bangermilton@hotmail.com

JOIN US ON THE FARM - HELP FEED THE ANIMALS

For a very child-friendly, highly recommended holiday, Torridge House Farm Cottages is where young families can join in helping to feed the animals: hens, ducks, pigs, rabbits, guinea pigs, mice and lots of young animals. The nine *VisitBritain* 3 and 4 Star quality cottages are welcoming, comfortable and well appointed. The small friendly, family-run farm has panoramic views of glorious Devon countryside with plenty of room to play in the large gardens, a heated outdoor summer swimming pool, barbecues, ball-play lawn, play room and games room. Torridge House Cottages have over 22 years experience of offering relaxed, hands on farm holidays. *To find out more please phone for a brochure or visit our website.*

TORRIDGE HOUSE FARM COTTAGES
LITTLE TORRINGTON, NORTH DEVON EX38 8PS
Tel: 01805 622542 • e-mail: holidays@torridgehouse.co.uk
www.torridgehouse.co.uk

Please note

All the information in this book is given in good faith in the belief that it is correct. However, the publishers cannot guarantee the facts given in these pages, neither are they responsible for changes in policy, ownership or terms that may take place after the date of going to press. Readers should always satisfy themselves that the facilities they require are available and that the terms, if quoted, still apply.

MANOR HOUSE & ASHBURY GOLF HOTELS

OKEHAMPTON · WEST DEVON

FREEPHONE 0800 234 3073

www.manorhousehotel.co.uk

Country House Hotel – Superb food, views and fantastic value breaks

Extensive sport and leisure facilities include:
7 x 18 hole golf courses · 6 indoor & 5 outdoor tennis courts · 13 lanes of indoor bowls
Guided walks on Dartmoor · Ranges – archery, air pistols and air rifles · Badminton, squash and short tennis · 3 x swimming pools, spa baths, saunas and steam room

ALL FREE OF CHARGE TO OUR RESIDENTS
Unique Craft Centre with 15 tutored crafts including:
Pottery · glass engraving · enamelling · jewellery making · picture framing
Beauty Treatments and Sports Massage including:
Indian head massage · aromatherapy · reflexology · swedish massage

WINTER BREAKS 3 nts £120/205; 4 nts £153/282 - XMAS BREAKS 4 nts from £458pp;
NEW YEAR BREAKS 3 nts from £369pp - SPRING BREAKS 3 nts £191/273; 4 nts £223/301
SUMMER BREAKS 3 nts £223/257; 4 nts £266/374
All breaks full board; child & group discounts

North Devon

Welcome to North Hill
deep in the rolling hills of Devon, a truly pastoral retreat

Carol Ann and Adrian Black, North Hill, Shirwell, Barnstaple EX31 4LG
Tel: 01271 850611
Mobile: 07834 806434
www.north-hill.co.uk

17th century farm buildings, sympathetically converted into cottages sleeping 2-6, with exposed beams, wood stoves and central heating. Set in 9 acres of pastures and gardens with a children's play area. Facilities include: indoor heated swimming pool, jacuzzi, sauna, all-weather tennis court and games room.

This area of North Devon offers some of the finest beaches in the country and the National Park of Exmoor offers thousands of acres of moorland to explore.

Terms from £195 to £965

Riverside Caravan & Camping Park
Marsh Lane, North Molton Road, South Molton EX36 3HQ

A beautiful, family-owned caravan and camping park in 40 acres of flat meadow and woodland near the market town of South Molton, an ideal base for exploring Exmoor.

- Luxurious heated shower and toilet block with free hot showers. • Laundry facilities and baby changing area. • Children and pets welcome.
- Specimen carp fishing lakes. • Coarse fishing lakes
- Barbecue and picnic tables.
- Hard standing, level Europitches.
- Electrical hook-up. • TV aerial sockets.
- Large open flat field available for rallies.

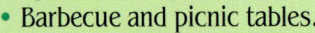

Tel: 01769 579269/574853
relax@exmoorriverside.co.uk
www.exmoorriverside.co.uk

Somerset & Wiltshire

SOMERSET & WILTSHIRE

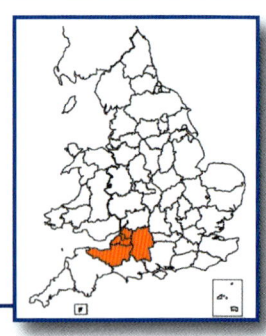

Best Beaches

There are some fine beaches in this delightful part of the country, including some of the West Country's most popular family holiday resorts. A Quality Coast Award has been gained once again by Burnham-on-Sea.

 South West Tourism
(Bristol & Bath, Cornwall, Devon, Dorset, Gloucestershire & The Cotswolds, Somerset, Wiltshire).

- **Tel: 0870 442 0880**
- **Fax: 0870 442 0881**
- **e-mail: info@swtourism.org.uk**
- **www.visitsouthwest.co.uk**

Some picturesque views from Wiltshire

Other specialised holiday guides from FHG
PUBS & INNS OF BRITAIN
COUNTRY HOTELS OF BRITAIN
WEEKEND & SHORT BREAKS
IN BRITAIN & IRELAND
THE GOLF GUIDE
WHERE TO PLAY, WHERE TO STAY
500 GREAT PLACES TO STAY IN BRITAIN
SELF-CATERING HOLIDAYS
BED & BREAKFAST STOPS IN BRITAIN
PETS WELCOME!
CARAVAN & CAMPING HOLIDAYS
IN BRITAIN

Published annually: available in all good bookshops or direct from the publisher:

e-mail: admin@fhguides.co.uk
www.holidayguides.com

Somerset & Wiltshire

MINEHEAD

Family Fun Activities: New look seafront with extensive sandy beach • Cruises and steam train rides • Horse riding and walking on nearby Exmoor • Theatre • Classic Car Collection • Butlins Family Entertainment Resort with a host of attractions including funfair, go karts, cinema, leisure pool and live shows.

Special Events: Late April/early May: Hobby Horse festivities. **July:** Minehead and Exmoor Festival; Friends of Thomas the Tank Engine Weekend.

Visitor Information Centre, Warren Road, Minehead TA24 5BG
01643 702624 • Fax: 01643 707166
e-mail: visitor@westsomerset.gov.uk
www.visit-exmoor.co.uk

Beaches

- **MINEHEAD STRAND BEACH.** Wide sandy beach with access down ramps from new sea wall. Ample parking. *Safety and maintenance:* cleaned daily. *Beach facilities:* cafe and takeaway food outlets; toilets with access. *Dog restrictions:* not allowed on beach from 1st May to 30th September; must be kept on lead on promenade.

- **MINEHEAD TERMINUS BEACH.** A mixture of sand and pebbles (continuation of the Strand in a westwards direction). *Facilities and Dog Restrictions:* as for Strand beach.

WESTON-SUPER-MARE

Family Fun Activities: The SeaQuarium • Grand Pier with amusements, land train, miniature railway, kids' play area • Marine lake • Donkey rides, amusements • Leisure centre • Tennis, putting, bowls, pitch and putt, ten-pin bowling, riding, rugby, football, cricket, fishing, golf • Cinema, museum, shows, night clubs, live music.

Special Events: for a full up-to-date listing of events visit **www.visitsomerset.co.uk** or call the Tourist Information Centre.

Events include national waterski races, Helidays, Sand Sculpture Festival, children's activities, Playhouse shows, motorcycle beach race and carnival.

Tourist Information Centre, Beach Lawns, Weston-super-Mare BS23 1AT
Tel: 01934 888800
Minicom: 01934 643172
westontouristinfo@n-somerset.gov.uk
www.visitsomerset.co.uk

Beaches

- **BEACH.** Two miles long, sandy with rock pools and shingle at Anchor Head. Promenade and piers; good parking. *Safety and maintenance:* beach cleaned daily all year. *Beach facilities:* deck chairs, donkeys and pony carts, marine lake and fun castle; ice-cream kiosks, snack bars, restaurants and pubs; toilets, some with access. *Dog restrictions:* dog ban on section of main beach between May and September.

Visit the FHG website **www.holidayguides.com**
for details of the wide choice of accommodation
featured in the full range of FHG titles

Somerset & Wiltshire

☆ Fun for all the Family ☆

◆ **Avon Valley Railway, near Bristol (0117 932 5538).** Working railway museum with locos and coaches. Enjoy a 5-mile trip along the lovely River Avon valley.
www.avonvalleyrailway.org

◆ **Bee World and Animal Centre, Stogumber (01984 656545).** Unravel the mysteries of bee-keeping and meet lots of friendly animals at this unique "hands-on" centre. Children's play area.

◆ **Bristol Zoo (0117 974 7399).** Extensive and fascinating collection including pygmy hippos and gorillas. Over 300 species from lions to dung beetles.
www.bristolzoo.org.uk

◆ **Cheddar Caves & Gorge (01934 742343).** Famous for its caves and underground pools, in a deep winding fissure in the Mendip Hills. Exhibitions and adventure walks.
www.chedddarcaves.co.uk

◆ **Cholderton Rare Breeds Farm Park, near Salisbury (01980 629438).** Rare and endangered breeds of British farm animals, plus Rabbit World with over 50 varieties. Pig racing (Pork Stakes) in peak season.
www.choldertoncharliesfarm.com

◆ **Wildlife Park at Cricket St Thomas, near Chard (01460 30111).** Large collection of wild animals and birds in 1000 acres of woodland and lakes.
www.wild.org.uk

◆ **Haynes Motor Museum, Sparkford, Near Yeovil (01963 440804).** Magnificent collection of over 250 vintage, veteran and classic cars, and 50 motorcycles. Experience 100 smiles per hour!
www.haynesmotormuseum.com

◆ **Longleat Safari Park, Warminster (01985 844400).** 100-acre reserve for lions, giraffes, monkeys, zebras and tigers roaming free. World's longest hedge maze, Postman Pat village.
www.longleat.co.uk

◆ **Brunel's SS Great Britain, Bristol (0117 926 0680).** Splendid six-masted ocean going vessel dating from 1843 and associated with engineering genius Isambard Kingdom Brunel.
www.ssgreatbritain.org

◆ **SeaQuarium, Weston-super-Mare (01934 613361).** Exciting close encounters with marvels of marine life, from starfish to sharks. Feeding demonstrations, talks and special presentations. New Rainforest River Zone.
www.seaquarium.co.uk

◆ **STEAM - Museum of Great Western Railway, Swindon (01793 466646).** Fun hands-on exhibits and rare archive footage tell the story of this famous railway company.
www.steam-museum.org.uk

◆ **West Somerset Railway, Bishops Lydeard (01643 704996).** A nostalgic journey through the unspoilt beauty of the Quantock Hills and along the coast; Visitor Centre and model railway.
www.west-somerset-railway.co.uk

◆ **Wookey Hole, Wells (01749 672243).** Britain's most spectacular caves, with dramatic lighting effects. Valley of the Dinosaurs, Monster Mill, Pirate Island Adventure golf, plus lots more.
www.wookey.co.uk

Somerset & Wiltshire

THE YARN MARKET HOTEL
High Street, Dunster TA24 6SF

The Yarn Market Hotel is a comfortable, family-run hotel which provides a friendly, relaxed atmosphere. Situated in the centre of a quaint English village, it is an ideal location for walking and exploring Exmoor, the surrounding coastline and the many local attractions. All rooms are en suite, with tea and coffee making facilities, and colour TV. Some have four-poster beds, while others have spectacular views over the surrounding countryside. Family rooms are also available. The restaurant offers a mouth-watering selection of dishes featuring local produce whenever possible. Packed lunches and drying facilities are also available. Non-smoking. Well-behaved pets are welcome. Party bookings and midweek breaks a speciality. B&B from £40.

Tel: 01643 821425   Fax: 01643 821475
e-mail: hotel@yarnmarkethotel.co.uk • www.yarnmarkethotel.co.uk

Sunfield
B and B Accommodation in Minehead

Delightful family-run private guest house only a few minutes' level walking distance from sea front

- Delicious home cooking • Full central heating
- 8 en suite bedrooms, all with courtesy tray, remote-control TV, hairdryer
- Children and well behaved pets welcome
- Totally non-smoking

83 Summerland Avenue, Minehead TA24 5BW
Tel: 01643 703565
www.sunfieldminehead.co.uk

Somerset & Wiltshire

Spinney Farmhouse ~ Thoulstone, Chapmanslade, Westbury BA13 4AQ

Off A36, three miles west of Warminster; 16 miles from historic city of Bath. Close to Longleat, Cheddar and Stourhead. Reasonable driving distance to Bristol, Stonehenge, Glastonbury and the cathedral cities of Wells and Salisbury. Pony trekking and fishing available locally.

- Washbasins, tea/coffee-making facilities and shaver points in all rooms.
- Family room available. • Guests' lounge with colour TV.
- Central heating. • Children and pets welcome.
- Ample parking. • Open all year. • No smoking

*Enjoy farm fresh food in a warm, friendly family atmosphere.
Bed and Breakfast from £25 per night. Reduction after 2 nights.
Evening Meal £12.*

Tel: 01373 832412 • e-mail: isabelandbob@btinternet.com

Primrose Hill

Primrose Hill offers spacious, comfortable accommodation in a terrace of four bungalows with private enclosed gardens and panoramic views over Blue Anchor Bay. The games room and boules pitch are popular with both adults and children. In walking distance of picturesque Blue Anchor Bay with its sandy beach, pubs, beachside cafes and indoor swimming pool. Within sight and sound of the West Somerset Railway.

Wheelchair-friendly • Dogs welcome • Internet connection

Winner Accessible Somerset 2008 and Exmoor Excellence Awards, 2006/2007

**Primrose Hill Holidays, Wood Lane, Blue Anchor TA24 6LA
Tel: 01643 821200 • info@primrosehillholidays.co.uk
www.primrosehillholidays.co.uk**

Please note

All the information in this book is given in good faith in the belief that it is correct. However, the publishers cannot guarantee the facts given in these pages, neither are they responsible for changes in policy, ownership or terms that may take place after the date of going to press. Readers should always satisfy themselves that the facilities they require are available and that the terms, if quoted, still apply.

Somerset & Wiltshire   57

A place to relax... for the holidaymaker who appreciates
peace and serenity, this friendly, family-run park is an ideal centre to explore Somerset, and is close to Devon and Cornwall's stunning coastline.
Easy access off B3141 • Open all year.
• Shower block with washing up area and chemical disposal point
• Well equipped amenity blocks • Electric hook-ups • Secure caravan storage
• Games room and children's play area
• WiFi available • Kitchen area with stainless steel tables, ice cube dispenser, microwaves, upright freezers • Shop with caravan accessories, toys and foodstuffs.

Fairways International Touring, Camping and Caravan Park
Bath Road, Bawdrip, Bridgwater, Somerset TA7 8PP
Tel/Fax: 01278 685569
e-mail: holiday@fairwaysinternational.co.uk
www.fairwaysinternational.co.uk

Somerset & Wiltshire

FOXHANGERS CANALSIDE FARM
Lower Foxhangers, Rowde, Devizes SN10 1SS
Tel & Fax: 01380 828254
e-mail: sales@foxhangers.co.uk • www.foxhangers.com

Small farm/marina with its many diverse attractions situated alongside the famous "Caen Hill" flights of 29 locks. Hear the near musical clatter of the windlass heralding the lock gate opening and the arrival of yet another colourful narrowboat. Relax on the patios of our rural retreats - four holiday mobile homes, all new models, sleeping 4/6. Ideally situated for fishing, cycling or walking. Pubs within easy walking distance. Short breaks when available. Secluded campsite nestling under the hedgerows, with electricity and facilities. Also narrowboat hire for weekly or short breaks. Avebury, Stonehenge, Bath and Longleat all close by

Colin and Cynthia Fletcher

Muchelney Ham Farm
Muchelney Ham, Langport TA10 0DJ

Self-catering cottage built in traditional style adjoining farmhouse. Double and family bedrooms, en suite. Large kitchen/diningroom. One further bathroom downstairs. Electricity by coin meter. Linen included in price.

Open all year
Weekly terms from £180 to £420.

Bed & Breakfast accommodation also available.

Tel: 01458 250737

www.muchelneyhamfarm.co.uk

Somerset & Wiltshire   59

ST AUDRIES BAY
Holiday Club

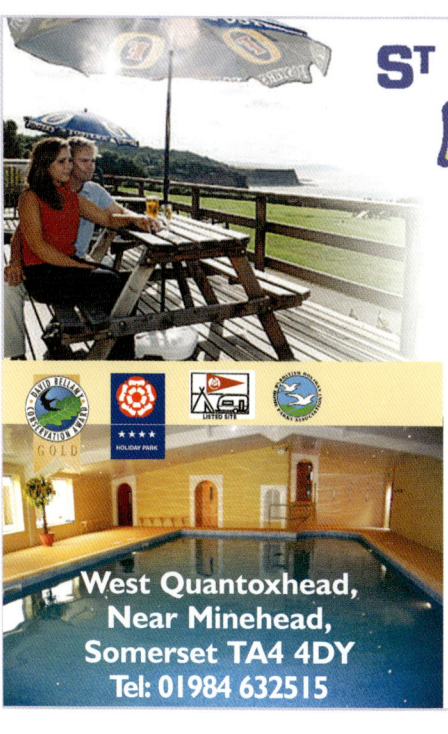

- Family-owned and run award-winning Park near Exmoor and The Quantocks
- 15 miles from the M5 • Fantastic views across the sea and beach access
- Sport & leisure facilities • Entertainment
- Licensed bars and restaurant
- Coffee Shop • On-site shop
- Children's play area
- Peaceful relaxing Park with family time in school holidays

Self-Catering & Half-Board Holidays
• Touring Caravans & Camping
• Luxury Holiday Homes for sale

West Quantoxhead,
Near Minehead,
Somerset TA4 4DY
Tel: 01984 632515

e-mail: info@staudriesbay.co.uk
www.staudriesbay.co.uk

Quantock Orchard Caravan Park

Award-winning, family-run campsite set amidst the stunning Somerset countryside.

Quantock Orchard is situated in an idyllic setting surrounded by picturesque views of the Quantocks, in an Area of Outstanding Natural Beauty. This peaceful park is close to Exmoor, the coast and the West Somerset Railway. Relax and unwind among these beautiful surroundings whilst enjoying our Five Star facilities.

• fully heated toilet and shower block • launderette • games room • adventure playground • shop • outdoor heated pool • gym with jacuzzi, steam room and sauna • cycle hire • caravan storage

Tents, tourers and motorhomes welcome
Luxury static holiday homes for sale or hire
Open all year

Michael & Sara Barrett,
Quantock Orchard Caravan Park, Flaxpool,
Crowcombe, Near Taunton TA4 4AW
01984 618618
e-mail: qocp@flaxpool.freeserve.co.uk
www.quantock-orchard.co.uk

DE LUXE PARK

Hampshire & Dorset

HAMPSHIRE & DORSET

 Best Beaches

No less than 11 beaches in the area have won European Blue Flag Awards for 2009.

[i] **South East England Tourism**
- Tel: 023 8062 5400
- Fax: 023 8062 0010
- e-mail: enquiries@tourismse.com
- www.visitsoutheastengland.com

BLUE FLAG BEACHES 2009
- **Bournemouth**
  Fisherman's Walk
  Alum Chine
  Durley Chine
  Southbourne
- **Poole**
  Canford Cliffs Chine
  Sandbanks
  Shore Road
  Branksome Chine
- **Swanage Central**
- **Hayling Island Central**
- **Hayling Island West**

[i] **South West Tourism**
(Bristol & Bath, Cornwall, Devon, Dorset, Gloucs & The Cotswolds, Somerset, Wiltshire).
- Tel: 0870 442 0880
- Fax: 0870 442 0881
- e-mail: info@swtourism.orguk
- www.visitsouthwest.co.uk

The view to the beach at Poole

For more information about holidaying in Dorset see:
- www.dorsetforyou.com
- www.westdorset.com (West Dorset)
- www.ruraldorset.com (North Dorset)
- www.dorset-newforest.com

For more information about holidaying in Hampshire see:
- www.vist-hampshire.co.uk

Hampshire & Dorset

BOURNEMOUTH

Family Fun Activities: Seven miles of golden sand, first-class attractions, beautiful gardens and summer festivals offer something for everyone from the Oceanarium to the Bournemouth International Centre and the Russell-Cotes Museum. There is plenty to do whatever the weather. Try the Bournemouth Eye tethered balloon ride.
Free 'Family Fun' brochure available on request from Visitor Information Bureau.

Special Events: **School Summer Holidays:** Kids Fun Festival with more than 100 free shows and activities. Sporting events, competitions and festivals take place throughout the year.

Visitor Information Bureau, Westover Road, Bournemouth BH1 2BU Information line and accommodation enquiries: 0845 0511700
e-mail: info@bournemouth.gov.uk
www.bournemouth.co.uk

Beaches

- **BEACH.** 7 miles long, sandy with traffic-free promenade, reached by zig-zag paths or cliff lifts. *Safety and maintenance:* lifeguard patrols, close-circuit TV surveillance, first-aid posts; cleaned twice daily. *Beach facilities:* children's beach GameZone in summer; rowing boats, pedalos, speed boats, kayaks, surfing; beach hut hire. "No Smoking" zones. Special 'Kidzone' safety areas. Excellent catering facilities. *Dog restrictions:* Dog-friendly sections of beach at Fisherman's Walk and Alum Chine between May and September inclusive; allowed on the promenade on lead.

POOLE

Family Fun Activities: Poole Quay with shops, crafts, museums, Poole Pottery with 'have a go area', restaurants • Crab lining, fishing trips, harbour boat trips, all types of watersports in Europe's largest natural harbour • Brownsea Island and road train • Poole Park with Gus Gorilla's indoor playground, crazy golf, Poole Park railway, mini icerink, outdoor playground, watersports • Tower Park Leisure Complex with cinema, Bowlplex, Splashdown, Monkey Bizness/Phazerzone, restaurants • Poole Museum with free entry • Sports centres with swimming, badminton, squash etc.
Free 'Family Fun' brochure and 'Treasure Hunt' available on request from Poole Welcome Centre.

Special Events: **May/September:** programme of spectacular weekday events featuring motorcycles, car nostalgia, fireworks, speedway, live entertainment, children's activities. **September:** Animal Windfest.

Poole Welcome Centre, Poole Quay, Poole BH15 1HJ • 01202 253253
e-mail: info@pooletourism.com
www.pooletourism.com

Beaches

- **BEACH.** Three miles of sands stretching from Sandbanks to Branksome Dene Chine. 7 car parks. *Safety and maintenance:* cleaned daily; lifeguard coverage in main season, beach station at Sandbanks manned throughout year. *Beach facilities:* beach huts, deckchairs and windbreaks for hire; watersports; ice-cream kiosks, snacks and cafe; toilets with facilities. *Dog restrictions:* banned from main beaches from May to September, must be kept on lead on promenade at all times.

Hampshire & Dorset

SWANAGE

Family Fun Activities: Bowling green, tennis, putting, crazy golf, 18-hole pitch and putt course, trampolines • Swanage Bay View Restaurant • Holiday park with swimming pool, skittle alley, indoor bowls and trimnasium • Water ski-ing, windsurfing, sailing, motor boats, sea angling • Castle, lighthouse, country park • Theatre/cinema.

Special Events: July: Swanage Jazz Festival. **August:** Regatta and Carnival Week. **September:** Swanage Folk Festival

Tourist Information Centre, Shore Road, Swanage BH19 1LB • 0870 4420680
e-mail: mail@swanage.gov.uk
www.swanage.gov.uk

Beaches

• **SWANAGE BAY BEACH.** Three miles long, sandy and naturally sheltered; promenade and good parking. *Safety and maintenance:* cleaned daily. *Beach facilities:* deck chairs, Punch and Judy; pedalcraft; toilets with & facilities. *Dog restrictions:* banned from main beach from 1st May to 30th September; must be kept on lead on promenade.

Crabbing at Poole

WEYMOUTH

Family Fun Activities: Country Park with Model World, Sea Life Park, Miniature Railway, Mini-Golf, Leisure Ranch and RSPB Nature Reserve • Weymouth Old Harbour including Brewers Quay Complex and Weymouth Timewalk, Sharky's, Nothe Fort and Gardens, Tudor House. • Pleasure cruises, float and boat hire, sailing, sub-aqua sports • Tennis, bowls • Swimming pool • Theatre with family shows, cinemas, night clubs • Superbowl

Special Events: May: Beach Kite Festival. **June:** Armed Forces Day Celebrations. **July:** RAF Careers Beach Volleyball Classic, Spirit of the Sea Festival. **August:** International Fireworks and Entertainment, Weymouth Carnival. **October:** Lions Club Beach Motocross.

Tourist Information Centre, The Esplanade, Weymouth • 01305 785747
weymouthtic@visitweymouth.co.uk
www.visitweymouth.co.uk

Beaches

• **WEYMOUTH BAY BEACH.** Two and a half miles long, sand running into shingle; promenade and piers. *Safety and maintenance:* Beach Control Centre, lifeguards; first aid and lost children post; beach cleaned daily. *Beach facilities:* donkey rides, deck chairs, Punch and Judy, trampolines, amusement arcades; floats, canoes; ice-cream kiosks, restaurants and pubs; toilets with & facilities. *Dog restrictions:* dogs restricted to special areas May-September.

FREE AND REDUCED RATE HOLIDAY VISITS!
Don't miss our Readers' Offer Vouchers on pages 163-180

Hampshire & Dorset 63

☆ Fun for all the Family ☆

◆ **Adventure Wonderland, Christchurch (01202 483444).** Guaranteed fun whatever the weather for 2-12 year olds. Also Wild Thing indoor play centre with themed and interactive equipment, and Alice Maze.
www.adventurewonderland.co.uk

◆ **Beaulieu (01590 612345).** National Motor Museum – motoring heritage brought back to life. Includes James Bond Experience. Also 13th century Abbey and Monastic Life exhibition.
www.beaulieu.co.uk

◆ **Blue Reef Aquarium, Portsmouth (02392 875222).** Innovative displays provide an insight into the mysterious world of the deep. Restaurant and children's attractions.
www.bluereefaquarium.co.uk

◆ **Dinosaur Museum, Dorchester (01305 269880).** Children of all ages love these scaly creatures, so make for this superb "hands on" exhibition dedicated entirely to dinosaurs.
www.thedinosaurmuseum.com

◆ **Longdown Activity Farm, Ashurst, Near Southampton (023 8029 2837).** Lots of hands-on activities every day, including small animal handling sessions, plus indoor and outdoor play areas. Gift shop and tearoom.
www.longdownfarm.co.uk

◆ **MarwellWildlife Park, near Winchester (01962 777407).** 200-acre park with rare wild animals including tigers, zebras, cheetahs, leopards, etc. Children's zoo, picnic area, cafe.
www.marwell.org.uk

◆ **New Forest Museum and Visitor Centre, Lyndhurst (023 8028 3444).** Learn the story of the Forest in an audio-visual show; gift shop specialising in local crafts.
www.newforestmuseum.org.uk

◆ **Paultons Park, near Romsey (023 8081 4442).** A fun-filled day out at this family leisure park with rides and thrills galore. Over 40 attractions/rides, including new Edge thrill ride.
www.paultonspark.co.uk

◆ **Tank Museum, Bovington, near Wareham (01929 405096).** Tanks and armoured cars from all over the world; "drive a tank" simulator; gift shop and restaurant.
www.tankmuseum.org

◆ **Teddy Bear Museum, Dorchester (01305 266040).** From the earliest antique teddy bears to today's TV favourites, they are all waiting to greet you. Collectors' shop, House with family of human-size bears.
www.teddybearhouse.co.uk

Visit the FHG website
www.holidayguides.com
for details of the wide choice of accommodation featured in the full range of FHG titles

Hampshire & Dorset

Southbourne Grove HOTEL

Friendly, family-run hotel with beautiful garden and ample guest parking. Close to beach and shops • Ideal position for exploring Bournemouth, Christchurch and the New Forest • Excellent breakfast served in spacious restaurant • En suite rooms, four-poster suite, ground floor rooms (one suitable for partially disabled) and large family bedrooms - all with Freeview TV and tea/coffee making facilities. Senior Citizen and Child discounts • Dogs welcome free of charge

B&B from £24 per night, from £140 per week.

This is a no-smoking hotel.

96 Southbourne Road, Southbourne, Bournemouth BH6 3QQ
Tel: 01202 420503 • Fax: 01202 421953
e-mail: neil@pack1462.freeserve.co.uk
http://tinyurl.com/koachs

Brambles
Bed & Breakfast accommodation in Dorset

Set in beautiful, tranquil countryside, Brambles is a pretty, thatched cottage offering every comfort, superb views and a friendly welcome. There is a choice of en suite, twin, double or single rooms, all very comfortable and with colour TV and tea/coffee making facilities. Pretty garden available for relaxing in. Full English or Continental breakfast served. Occasional evening meals available by arrangement. Parking available. There are many interesting places to visit and wonderful walks for enthusiasts. B&B from £25 single pppn, £35 double/twin pppn.

**Woolcombe, Melbury Bubb, Dorchester DT2 0NJ
Tel: 01935 83672 • www.bramblesdorset.co.uk
e-mail: bramblesbandb@hotmail.co.uk**

Hampshire & Dorset

••Lulworth Cove••
Cromwell House Hotel

Catriona and Alistair Miller welcome guests to their comfortable family-run hotel, set in secluded gardens with spectacular sea views. Situated 200 yards from Lulworth Cove, with direct access to the Jurassic Coast. Accommodation is in 20 en suite bedrooms, with TV, direct-dial telephone, wi-fi, and tea/coffee making facilities; most have spectacular sea views. There is disabled access and a room suitable for disabled guests.
• Self-catering flat and cottage available. • Restaurant, bar wine list.
• A heated swimming pool is available from May to October.

**Cromwell House Hotel,
Lulworth Cove BH20 5RJ**
Tel: 01929 400253/400332 • Fax: 01929 400566

www.lulworthcove.co.uk

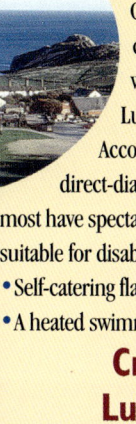

71 Wakeham, Easton, Portland DT5 1HW

The Alessandria is situated on the Isle of Portland, about three miles southwest from Weymouth, and in the heart of Dorset. The hotel comprises 15 comfortable guest rooms, including two on the ground floor with disabled/mobility access. Some rooms have glorious sea views out towards the famous Portland Bill and to the Channel.

Quiet location • Free parking • Bed & Breakfast at good prices
En suite • Tea coffee making facilities • Colour TV

The Alessandria has been under the management of proprietor Giovanni Bisogno for 20 years, and is highly recommended by our guests. Many guests return again and again for the 'home from home' comfort and friendly, good old-fashioned service and value.

Tel: Giovanni 01305 822270 • Fax: 01305 820561
www.alessandriahotel.co.uk

The Alessandria

Hampshire & Dorset

This handsome 18th century stone barn is situated in some of the most picturesque of Dorset's countryside. Set in its own secluded, landscaped gardens, the barn has been extensively modernised to provide high quality accommodation at affordable prices.

There are two large en suite guest suites on the second floor and a third suite on the ground floor with disabled access. The rooms are all newly refurbished to a high standard, each with television, hairdryer, footspa and hospitality tray. Heated outdoor swimming pool in grounds.

Stoneleigh Barn

Mrs Penny Smith.

**North Wootton, Sherborne DT9 5JW
Tel: 01935 815964
www.stoneleighbarn.com
e-mail: stoneleighbarn@aol.com**
Please quote 'FHG'

Poole, Dorset

Hampshire & Dorset

THE KNOLL HOUSE
STUDLAND BAY

A peaceful oasis and wonderful atmosphere where families matter

~

Easy access to three miles of golden beach
Outdoor pool (level deck), golf and tennis for all ages
Health Spa with plunge pool and sauna

~

Connecting rooms for families with children
Separate younger children's restaurant
Playroom and fabulous Adventure Playground

~

Open Easter - end November. Dogs also welcome

STUDLAND BAY
DORSET
BH19 3AH
01929 · 450450
info@knollhouse.co.uk
www.knollhouse.co.uk

ONLY 2 HOURS FROM HEATHROW

Hampshire & Dorset

DISCOVER RELAX EXPLORE UNWIND ENJOY

Have you heard about Shorefield Holidays?

All four of our holiday parks offer self-catering accommodation and are set in peaceful, unspoilt parkland in the beautiful South Coast area.

There is a choice of luxury caravans or timber lodges depending on which park you choose. There are comprehensive leisure facilities available and great entertainment for the whole family. Pamper yourself in our 'Reflections' Day Spa at Shorefield Country Park, explore the New Forest National Park, or relax on Bournemouth's sandy beaches.

For full details, ask for our brochure or browse online.

Tel 01590 648331

holidays@shorefield.co.uk
www.shorefield.co.uk   Ref: FHG

HAMPSHIRE

Shorefield Country Park
Milford on Sea, SO41 0LH

Oakdene Forest Park
St. Leonards, BH24 2RZ

Forest Edge Holiday Park
St. Leonards, BH24 2SD

DORSET

Swanage Coastal Park
Swanage, BH19 2RS

Hampshire & Dorset

Orchard End & The Old Coach House
Hooke, Beaminster, Dorset

Orchard End is a stone-built bungalow, with electric central heating and double glazing. Four bedrooms, two bathrooms; sleeps 8. Well-equipped and comfortable. Enclosed garden and off-road parking.

For details contact: Mrs Pauline M. Wallbridge, Watermeadow House, Hooke, Beaminster, Dorset DT8 3PD • Tel: /Fax: 01308 862619

Hooke is a quiet village nine miles from the coast. Good walking country and near Hooke Working Woodland with lovely woodland walks. Coarse fishing nearby. Terms from £300 to £750 inclusive of VAT, electricity, bed linen and towels.
enquiries@watermeadowhouse.co.uk • www.watermeadowhouse.co.uk

Both properties ETC ★★★

The Old Coach House, a cottage sleeping 9, is also finished to a high standard. Four bedrooms, two bathrooms; central heating. Large garden; off-road parking. Both properties (on a working dairy farm) are equipped with washing machine, dryer, dishwasher, fridge/freezers, microwaves and payphones.

BOURNEMOUTH HOLIDAY APARTMENTS

Proprietors Mike and Lyn Lambert have been catering for Bournemouth holidaymakers at Aaron and Lyttelton Lodge for over 35 years. These modern holiday apartments situated in a pleasant residential area of Boscombe offer accommodation for 1-10 persons in clean self-catering studios, one, two and four bedroom flats close to a superb sandy beach, shops and entertainments.

Holidaymakers are accommodated in either an elegant Victorian property or spacious new wing. Each flat is completely self-contained and provided with constant hot water from each flat's own gas boiler.

Bournemouth town centre is a few minutes away by car or there is a frequent bus service. A car parking space is provided for each apartment in our own grounds. Boscombe is an ideal base for touring many places of interest in the Dorset and Hampshire countryside, with to the east, the New Forest, Beaulieu and the Isle of Wight, and to the west, Poole with its magnificent harbour, Corfe Castle, the Jurassic coast and the picturesque Dorset villages.

**16 Florence Road,
Bournemouth BH5 1HF
Tel: 01202 304925**

**www.selfcateringbournemouth.co.uk
e-mail: mikelyn_lambert@btinternet.com**

Hampshire & Dorset

Cardsmill
Farm Holidays

Whitchurch Canonicorum,
Charmouth, Bridport,
Dorset DT6 6RP
Tel & Fax: 01297 489375
e-mail: cardsmill@aol.com
www.farmhousedorset.com

Stay on a real working family farm in the Marshwood Vale, an Area of Outstanding Natural Beauty. Enjoy country walks to the village, coast and around farm and woods. Watch the daily milking, see baby calves and lambs, and seasonal activities here on this 590 acre farm. En suite family, double and twin rooms available, with CTV, tea/coffee trays.
B&B £28-£36pppn. ETC ★★★★ *(inspected March 2009)*

Also available, three large, rural, quiet farmhouses. Each has private garden, double glazed conservatory and ample parking.
• TAPHOUSE has 6 bedrooms, 4 bathrooms, lounge, 22'x15' kitchen/diner.
• COURTHOUSE COTTAGE and DAIRY each have 3/4 bedrooms and 2 or 3 bathrooms. Games room, parking, separate gardens. All have C/H, dishwasher, washing machine and very well equipped kitchen/diner/lounge.
All available all year for long or short stays.
Brochure available, or check the website.

WELCOME TO HAYLING ISLAND
FAMILY CAMP SITES

Hayling Island is an ideal touring base for Portsmouth, the Isle of Wight and the New Forest, with excellent motorway access.
We have safe, clean, award-winning beaches, and windsurfing, sailing, horse riding, golf, tennis and walking to be enjoyed locally.

Our campsite has children's play areas, electric hook-ups, toilets and hot water, heated swimming pool.
Many other extras included.

The Oven Campsite
Tel: 023 9246 4695 • Mobile: 077584 10020
e-mail: theovencampsite@talktalk.net
www.haylingcampsites.co.uk

Hampshire & Dorset

FREE AND REDUCED RATE HOLIDAY VISITS!
Don't miss our
Readers' Offer Vouchers
on pages 163-180

Littlesea Holiday Park, Weymouth
✔ 5 Star Park
✔ Kids Clubs
✔ Entertainment
✔ Great Location
✔ Heated Indoor & Outdoor Pools
✔ Outdoor Family FunZone
✔ Tourers Welcome

FANTASTIC OFFERS THROUGHOUT THE YEAR

Quote: FHG **Haven**
Call **0871 231 0879** www.littlesea-park.co.uk
*Subject to availability. Full T&C's apply. Minimum call charges apply.

Tamarisk Farm
Beach Road, West Bexington, Dorchester DT2 9DF
Tel: 01308 897784   Mrs Josephine Pearse

On slope overlooking Chesil beach between Abbotsbury and Burton Bradstock.
Three large (Mimosa is wheelchair disabled M3(i), Granary Lodge is disabled-friendly (M1) and The Moat) and two small cottages (VB 3/4 Stars). Each one stands in own fenced garden.
Glorious views along West Dorset and Devon coasts. Lovely walks by sea and inland. Part of mixed organic farm with arable, sheep, cattle, horses and market garden (organic vegetables, meat and wholemeal flour available). Sea fishing, riding in Portesham and Burton Bradstock, lots of tourist attractions and good markets. Good centre for touring Thomas Hardy's Wessex. Safe for children and excellent for dogs. Very quiet. Terms from £260 to £980.
e-mail: holidays@tamariskfarm.com • • www.tamariskfarm.com/holidays

Mimosa — *The Fossil & The Cross* — *Granary Lodge*

Woolsbridge Manor Farm caravan park

Three Legged Cross,
Wimborne, Dorset BH21 6RA
Telephone: 01202 826369

Your base for exploring Dorset and the New Forest

Situated approximately three-and-a-half-miles from the New Forest market town of Ringwood – easy access to the south coast. Seven acres level, semi-sheltered, well-drained spacious pitches. Quiet country location on a working farm, ideal and safe for families. Showers, mother/baby area, laundry room, washing up area, chemical disposal, payphone, electric hook-ups, battery charging. Children's play area on site. Site shop. Dogs welcome on leads. Fishing adjacent.
Moors Valley Country Park golf course one mile. Pub and restaurant 10 minutes' walk.

e-mail: woolsbridge@btconnect.com • www.woolsbridgemanorcaravanpark.co.uk

ISLE OF WIGHT

Best Beaches

The varied coastline of the Isle of Wight includes many safe, sandy beaches. Colwell, Cowes, East Cowes, Gurnard, Ryde East, Seagrove, Shanklin, Springvale, Totland Bay and Yaverland have won a Quality Coast Award, and two beaches have earned the right to fly a Blue Flag.

BLUE FLAG BEACHES 2009
- Sandown
- Ventnor

i **Isle of Wight Tourism**
- Tel: 01983 813813
- Fax: 01983 823031
- e-mail: info@islandbreaks.co.uk
- www.islandbreaks.co.uk

Ryde, Seaview & St Helens

 Family Fun Activities: Boating lake, bowling alley, swimming pool, ice skating rink, cinema • Dotto train along seafront and into town • Seaview Wildlife Encounter where children can hand-feed penguins, macaws and parrots • Travel back in time on the Isle of Wight Steam Railway.

☆ **Special Events:** **July:** Ryde Regatta. **August/September:** Ryde Carnival.

 Beaches

• **BEACH.** Coastline three-and-a-half miles long; sand at Ryde, rockpools at Seaview; ample parking. *Safety and maintenance:* inshore rescue; cleaned daily. *Beach facilities:* canoe lake on esplanade, swimming pools, playground, mini fun fair, trampolines; snack bars and restaurants (some licensed); toilets with ♿ access. *Dog restrictions:* banned on main areas of beach from 1st May to 30th September; must be kept on lead on promenade; "poop scoop" regulations in force.

Sandown & Lake

 Family Fun Activities: Fishing, tennis, basketball, putting, pitch and putt, crazy golf • Pier with bowling and other attractions • Street market • Zoo • Leisure centre • Dinosaur Isle • Dotto train • Go-karts.

Isle of Wight

⭐ **Special Events:** **July/August:** Carnival. **August:** Regatta.

🏖 Beaches

• **BEACH.** Approximately three miles long, sandy with cliffs at back; promenade, pier complex with bar, restaurant, amusements. *Safety and maintenance:* warning flags, lifeguards; cleaned daily in season. Kidzone in selected parts. *Beach facilities:* deck chairs, windsurfing, pedalcraft, children's entertainment; snack bars on promenade open during summer season; toilets with ♿ access. *Dog restrictions:* banned from main areas of beach from 1st May to 30th September; "poop scoop" regulations in force.

Ventnor

🏛 **Family Fun Activities:** Botanic Gardens and Winter Gardens with regular entertainment • Golf • Marina • Nearby Blackgang Chine has attractions and rides for the whole family.

⭐ **Special Events:** **August:** Carnival.

🏖 Beaches

• **BEACH.** Approximately quarter-of-a-mile long; mainly sand, some shingle; promenade. *Safety and maintenance:* cleaned daily. *Beach facilities:* deck chairs; snack bars and restaurants, amusements; public house; toilets with ♿ access. *Dog restrictions:* banned on main beach areas from 1st May to 30th September; "poop scoop" regulations in force.

Colwell & Totland

Small resort on Totland Bay, three miles south-west of Yarmouth.

• **BEACH.** One-and-a-half miles long; sandy at Colwell, sand with some shingle at Totland; sea wall connects the two bays. *Safety and maintenance:* partly cleaned daily in season. *Beach facilities:* deck chairs and paddlecraft at Colwell; snacks and ice-cream at both locations. *Dog restrictions:* not allowed on Colwell beach between 1st May and 30th September.

Shanklin

🏛 **Family Fun Activities:** Water activities • Indoor play area, crazy golf, golf, putting • Dotto train • Cliff lift to esplanade.

⭐ **Special Events:** Shanklin Theatre shows. **August:** Shanklin Town regatta and sea events.

🏖 Beaches

• **BEACH.** Sandy beach, access via cliff lift; two-mile long promenade connects town to Sandown. Shanklin Chine illuminated on summer evenings. *Beach facilities:* refreshments, toilets; deck chairs, beach huts. *Dog restrictions:* banned from main beach from 1st May to 30th September.

Yarmouth

One of the oldest towns on the Island with a busy harbour. Boat trips to Needles from pier. Nearby attractions include Fort Victoria, Dimbola Lodge and Dinosaur Farm Museum.

⭐ **Special Events:** **May/June:** Yarmouth Old Gaffers Festival.

🏖 Beaches

• **BEACH.** Shingle beach with pier; swimming at Sandhard area. *Beach facilities:* refreshments; toilets. *Dog restrictions:* must be kept on lead.

FHG Guides

74 **Isle of Wight**

Frenchman's Cove
Alum Bay Old Road, Totland, Isle of Wight PO39 0HZ

Our delightful family-run guesthouse is set amongst National Trust downland, not far from the Needles and safe sandy beaches. Ideal for ramblers, birdwatchers, cyclists and those who enjoy the countryside

We have almost an acre of grounds. Cots and high chairs are available. All rooms are en suite, with colour TV and tea/coffee making facilities. Four ground floor bedrooms suitable for most disabled guests. Guests can relax in the attractive lounges.

Also available is the Coach House, a well appointed self-catering apartment for two adults and two children. No smoking. No pets.

Please contact Sue or Chris Boatfield for details.
Tel: 01983 752227
www.frenchmanscove.co.uk

☆ Fun for all the Family ☆

◆ **Amazon World, Newchurch (01983 867122).** All-weather Amazon Rain Forest attraction with over 200 species of birds and animals. Falconry displays.
www.amazonworld.co.uk

◆ **Blackgang Chine, Chale (01983 730052).** 40 acres of cliff top gardens, exhibitions, fantasy attractions – Cowboy Town, Nurseryland, Giant Snakes 'n' Ladders, Water Force, a 100m high speed boat ride.
www.blackgangchine.com

◆ **Dinosaur Isle, Sandown (01983 404344).** Exciting new exhibition centre in a spectacular pterosaur-shaped building, with life-size dinosaurs; guided fossil walks to sites of interest on the island.
www.dinosaurisle.com

◆ **Isle of Wight Steam Railway, Near Ryde (01983 882204).** 5-mile round trip on genuine vintage train. Station at Havenstreet with museum, shop, cafe and bar.
www.iwsteamrailway.co.uk

◆ **Brading The Experience (01983 407286).** World-famous museum set in 11th century rectory mansion. Visit the Chamber of Horrors and Animal World.
www.bradingtheexperience.co.uk

◆ **Natural History Centre, Godshill (01983 840333).** A fascinating display of tropical seashells, birds, butterflies and even a lizard embalmed in amber, all housed in a 17th century coach house.
www.shellmuseum.co.uk

Isle of Wight

Island Cottage Holidays

Self Catering Holiday Cottage accommodation on the Isle of Wight

More than 75 charming individual cottages situated throughout the island, in lovely rural surroundings and close to the sea.

- Thatched cottages • Cottages with sea views or with short walk to the sea
- Larger cottages • Cottages accepting dogs and pets • Gold award cottages

Beautiful views, attractive gardens, delightful country walks.

All equipped to a high standard and graded for quality by the Tourist Board ★★★ to ★★★★★

For a brochure please **Tel: (01929) 480080 • Fax: (01929) 481070**
e-mail: enq@islandcottageholidays.com
www.islandcottageholidays.com

Open all year (Sleep 1 - 12) £185– £1595 per week. Short breaks available in low season (3 nights) £155 – £399

Ventnor Holiday Villas

The apartments and villas are on a south-facing hillside leading down to a small rocky bay. The sea views are spectacular and the hillside sheltered, but open to all the sunshine that is going.

Villas sleep two to six, apartments sleep four.
Caravans also available, sleeping four.

Colour TV, no extra charge for linen. Free cots and high chairs. Car parking, sea view. Villas and caravans open April to October, apartments open all year. Three-night break per unit from £195. Pets welcome in villas. Write or phone for brochure.

Mr King
Ventnor Holiday Villas
Wheelers Bay Road
Ventnor
Isle of Wight PO38 1HR
sales@ventnorholidayvillas.co.uk
www.ventnorholidayvillas.co.uk
Tel: 01983 852973

Sussex

SUSSEX

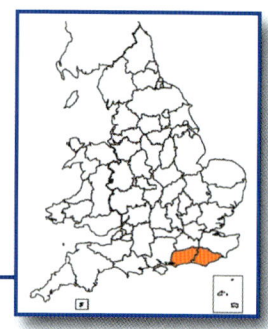

Best Beaches

Three beaches on this lively stretch of coast have earned 2009 Blue Flag awards after meeting a variety of strict criteria.

BLUE FLAG BEACHES 2009
- West Wittering
- Littlehampton Coastguards
- West Street

 South East England Tourism
- **Tel: 023 8062 5400**
- **Fax: 023 8062 0010**
- **e-mail: enquiries@tourismse.com**
- **www.visitsoutheastengland.com**

Falling Sands, Eastbourne

For more information about holidaying in Sussex see:
- www.visitsussex.org • www.sussexbythesea.com • www.eastsussex.gov.uk

Sussex

BRIGHTON

Family Fun Activities: Brighton Pier, Sea Life Centre, Royal Pavilion, Brighton Museum, British Engineerium, Preston Manor, Foredown Tower, West Blatchington Windmill, Fishing Museum, National Museum of Penny Slot Machines; Marina Village • Fishing, boat trips, windsurfing, sailing • Horse racing, greyhound racing • 10-pin bowling, putting, crazy golf, pitch and putt, golf courses, skate boarding, roller blading, ice skating, tennis, squash, bowls, badminton, cycle hire, indoor swimming pools • Cinemas, theatres, nightclubs, discos • Churchill Square, North Laine and Lanes shopping districts with family-friendly restaurants and cafes.

Special Events: May: Brighton Festival. **June:** London-Brighton Bike Ride. **July:** Kite Festival. **August:** Circus. **November:** Veteran Car Run.

VisitBrighton, Royal Pavilion Shop, 4-5 Pavilion Buildings, Brighton BN1 1EE 0906 711 2255
brighton-tourism@brighton-hove.gov.uk
www.visitbrighton.com

Beaches

• BEACH. 7 miles long, shingle and rockpools; cliff walk, promenade with Volks Railway, pier with funfair and arcades. Artists' and fishing quarters. Naturist area at eastern end of promenade, near marina; warning flags, lifeguards (some undertow at extreme eastern end); cleaned daily in season. *Beach facilities:* deck chairs; ramp and lift to lower promenade; paddling pool, new children's play area; volleyball, basketball; showers; ice-cream kiosks, snack bars, restaurants and pubs; toilets with ♿ access, baby changing facilities. *Dog restrictions:* dogs allowed from West Pier to Hove boundary and from Volks Railway to Banjo Groyne. Not allowed on any other part of the beach.

BOGNOR REGIS

Family Fun Activities: Free summer Sunday afternoon bandstand concerts in Hotham Park • Playgrounds, amusement arcades, tennis, putting, crazy golf, golf course, sailing • Cinema • Day visitors welcome at Butlins Family Entertainment Centre • Miniature railway in Hotham Park.

Special Events: Various events throughout the summer including: Bognor Birdman (the original), Sands of Time Seaside Festival, Illumination Gala and Procession, Here Comes Summer.

Visitor Information Centre, Belmont Street, Bognor Regis • 01243 823140
e-mail: bognorregis.vic@arun.gov.uk
www.sussexbythesea.com

Beaches

• BEACH. 8 miles long, sand and shingle, naturally sheltered; promenade and pier with arcades; ample voucher parking. *Safety and maintenance:* warning signs, rocks at low tide; cleaned regularly. *Beach facilities:* deck chairs, showers, children's play area; Kidcare Scheme along 50-metre stretch of seafront; seafront landtrain; ice-cream kiosks, snack bars, restaurants, pubs; toilets (toilets with ♿ access on sea front). *Dog restrictions:* not allowed on main beach from May to September.

FREE AND REDUCED RATE HOLIDAY VISITS!
Don't miss our
Readers' Offer Vouchers
on pages 163-180

Sussex

EASTBOURNE

Family Fun Activities: Fort Fun and Treasure Island theme parks, Miniature Steam Railway, Sovereign Centre, Knockhatch Adventure Park, Drusillas Zoo, Seven Sisters Sheep Centre, Museum of Shops, Redoubt Fortress, Lifeboat Museum, historic Pevensey Castle and Michelham Priory, Victorian Pier with arcades, family pub and Camera Obscura • Multiplex cinema, four theatres, seafront bandstand, indoor karting, 10-pin bowling, tennis, mini-golf, Dotto Train, speedway stadium.

Special Events: May: Magnificent Motors. **June:** Classic Motorcycle Run, International Tennis Championships **July:** Emergency Services Display. **August:** International Air Show, Family Festival of Tennis, Tennis championships; South of England Tennis championships. **September:** MG South Downs Run. **October:** Victorian Festival, Beer Festival.

 Tourist Information Centre, Cornfield Road, Eastbourne BN21 4QA
0871 663 0031
e-mail: tic@eastbourne.gov.uk
www.visiteastbourne.com

Beaches

• **BEACH.** Five miles of beaches; shingle, sand and rockpools; promenade and pier with arcades, seafront cycleway; Dotto Train service; ample parking. *Safety and maintenance:* warning flags, lifeguards; Kidzone wristband scheme, first aid, rookie lifeguard classes. *Beach facilities:* deck chairs, sun loungers, parasols, beach huts, paddlecraft, water sports, boat trips, seafront bandstand, Punch & Judy; ice-cream kiosks, snack bars, restaurants and pubs; showers, toilets with ♿ access and baby changing facilities.

Sailing at Eastbourne

Sussex

★ Fun for all the Family ★

◆ **1066 Battle Abbey and Battlefield, Battle (01424 775705).** Founded by William the Conqueror to commemorate the Battle of Hastings in 1066. The battle site, Abbey ruins and grounds are open to the public.
www.english-heritage.org.uk

◆ **Bentley Wildfowl and Motor Museum, near Lewes (01825 840573).** Hundreds of waterfowl and wildlife, including flamingos, cranes and peacocks, in 23 acres.
www.bentley.org.uk

◆ **Bluebell Railway, near Uckfield (01825 720800).** Collection of veteran locos from 1865 to 1958. Trains steam through miles of Sussex countryside.
www.bluebell-railway.co.uk

◆ **Buckley's Yesterday's World, Battle (01424 775378).** Experience a day in a bygone age and explore the re-created shop and room displays. Children's activity areas, gift shop, teas.
www.yesterdaysworld.co.uk

◆ **Drusillas Park, Alfriston (01323 874100).** Award-winning attraction with collection of rare cattle, exotic flamingos, waterfowl, monkeys and parrots. Farm playground, miniature railway, shops.
www.drusillas.co.uk

◆ **Earnley Butterflies & Gardens, Near Chichester (01243 512637).** Walk amongst amazing tropical butterflies, stroll through themed gardens, and explore life as it used to be in the Nostalgia Museum.
www.earnleybutterfliesandgardens.co.uk

◆ **Paradise Park, Newhaven (01273 512123).** Journey through time and see how plants and animals lived 200 million years ago. Miniature railway, gnome settlement.
www.paradisepark.co.uk

◆ **Royal Pavilion, Brighton (03000 290900).** The former seaside palace of George IV, with lavish Chinese-style interiors. Shop and tearoom.
www.royalpavilion.org.uk

◆ **Sea Life Centre Brighton (01273 604234).** Come face to face with thousands of fascinating sea creatures. Restaurants and shops.
www.sealife.co.uk

◆ **Seven Sisters Sheep Centre, Near Eastbourne (01323 423302).** Over 40 breeds of sheep - help feed the lambs in Spring, see the sheep being milked, or take a ride on the tractor trailer. We'll be pleased to meet 'ewe'!
www.sheepcentre.co.uk

◆ **Smugglers Adventure, Hastings (01424 444412).** Relive the dangers and excitement that faced smugglers and customs men in times past. Displays and tableaux with life-sized figures.
www.smugglersadventure.co.uk

◆ **Weald and Downland Open Air Museum, near Chichester (01243 811363).** A collection of historic buildings, 16th century treadwheel etc saved from destruction. Heavy horses, shop, cafe.
www.wealddown.co.uk

Sussex

BUXTED PARK COUNTRY HOUSE • Buxted, Uckfield, E. Sussex TN22 4AY
Tel: 01825 733333 • www.handpickedhotels.co.uk

In the heart of Sussex, this magnificent country house hotel is set in 300 acres of parkland, yet conveniently close to Gatwick, Brighton & Hove.
Family rooms • Baby listening • Babysitting • Play area / games • Bottle warming

The Grand Hotel • King Edward's Parade, Eastbourne, E. Sussex BN21 4EQ
Tel: 01323 412345 • www.grandeastbourne.com

This child-friendly hotel offers a wide variety of amenities, including a supervised programme of events to keep the kids amused while you take advantage of the superb leisure facilities.
Family rooms • Interconnecting rooms • Play area / games • Bottle warming

BAILIFFSCOURT HOTEL & HEALTH SPA • Climping Street, Climping, Littlehampton, W. Sussex BN17 5RW • 01903 723511 • www.hshotels.co.uk

This classic manor house near Climping beach is the perfect place for family holidays. Gardens, swimming pools, sports facilities and even an early children's menu in the evening so parents can enjoy a quiet dinner later!
Family rooms • Interconnecting rooms • Baby listening • Bottle warming

BRAMBLE COTTAGE • The Street, Bolney, W. Sussex RH17 5PG
Tel: 01444 881643 • www.bramblecottagebb.co.uk

In quiet village, central for many local attractions; near Burgess Hill, Haywards Heath, Gatwick Airport, and Brighton. Friendly, family-run establishment, serving good English breakfasts. All rooms have en suite or private facilities. Two local pubs/restaurants within walking distance.

CROWHURST PARK
Holiday Village

**Telham Lane
Battle
East Sussex
TN33 0SL
Tel: 01424 773344**

Award-winning holiday park featuring luxury log cabin accommodation. Magnificent heated pool complex with children's paddling area, Jacuzzi, steam room, sauna, gym with cardiovascular and resistance training equipment, beauty therapies, aquafit classes, tennis court, children's adventure play area, restaurant, bars and clubhouse. All this plus beautiful, historic 1066 Country on your doorstep and the Sussex coast just five miles away.
Call for a brochure today.
enquiries@crowhurstpark.co.uk
www.crowhurstpark.co.uk

KENT

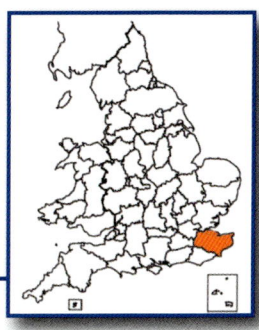

Best Beaches

[i] South East England Tourism
- Tel: 023 8062 5400
- Fax: 023 8062 0010
- e-mail: enquiries@tourismse.com
- www.visitsoutheastengland.com

A record number of beaches on the Kent coast have gained the prestigious Blue Flag Award for the highest standards of beach management and cleanliness.

BLUE FLAG BEACHES 2009
- Birchington Minnis Bay
- St Mildreds Bay, Westgate
- West Bay Westgate
- Botany Bay, Westgate
- Ramsgate Main Sands
- Joss Bay

For more information about holidaying in Kent see:
- www.visitkent.co.uk
- www.heartofkent.org.uk
- www.kentattractions.co.uk

Ramsgate Harbour

BROADSTAIRS

Family Fun Activities: Ice-cream parlours, amusement arcade, Pavilion with all-year entertainment, bandstand • Tennis, putting, golf course, crazy golf, bowls, angling, sailing • Award-winning St Peter's Village Tour • Skate park and climbing centre • Dickens House, Crampton Tower Museum.

Special Events: June: Dickens Festival Week. **July:** Sea Sunday. **August:** Water Gala Day. Folk Week **September:** Open Bowls Tournament.

i Visitor Information Centre, (in Dickens House Museum), 2 Victoria Parade, Broadstairs CT10 1QS
0870 264 6111
e-mail: tourism@thanet.gov.uk
www.visitthanet.co.uk

Beaches

- **VIKING BAY.** Sandy beach, 150 metres long; promenade, harbour, pier and boardwalk, parking; access. *Safety and maintenance:* first-aid station, warning flags, animal logo signposts; lifeguards, bay inspector/information; cleaned daily. *Beach facilities:* deck chairs/sun loungers and chalets for hire, children's rides, donkey rides, Punch and Judy (August only); pubs, cafes, shops and restaurants nearby, amusements, surfski/belly boards; lift to beach; toilets Broadstairs Harbour and Victoria Gardens). *Dog restrictions:* not permitted on beach 1 May to 30 September incl.

- **STONE BAY.** 200 metres long, sandy with chalk cliffs and rockpools; promenade; access. *Safety and maintenance:* cleaned daily; lifeguards. *Beach facilities:* chalets for hire. Cafes and restaurants nearby. Toilets. *Dog restrictions:* banned 1 May to 30 September between 10am and 6pm.

- **LOUISA BAY.** 150 metres long, quiet sandy bay; promenade. Disabled access via fairly steep slope. *Safety and maintenance:* warning signs; beach cleaned daily. *Beach facilities:* chalets for hire; cafe, tidal pool. *Dog restrictions:* not permitted 10am-6pm 1 May-30 Sept

- **JOSS BAY.** 200 metres long, sandy beach, parking, access. *Safety and maintenance:* warning flags, lifeguards; cleaned daily; animal logo signposts to help children find their way back to parents. *Beach facilities:* deck chairs for hire, surf skis/belly boards; lessons; cafe; toilets with RADAR key access Easter-Sep. *Dog restrictions:* not permitted 10am-6pm 1 May-30 Sept; "poop scoop" beach.

- **KINGSGATE BAY.** 150 metres long; quiet and secluded sandy beach. *Safety and maintenance:* cleaned daily. *Beach facilities:* chalets for hire; clifftop pub. *Dog restrictions:* "poop scoop" beach.

- **BOTANY BAY.** 200 metres long, sandy beach; access. *Safety and maintenance:* lifeguards/bay inspector; warnings, cleaned daily. *Beach facilities:* cafe, clifftop pub; toilets. *Dog restrictions:* not permitted 10am-6pm 1 May-30 Sept.

- **DUMPTON GAP.** Quiet sandy bay with some rocks, 150 metres long; promenade and parking. Disabled access. *Safety and maintenance:* warning signs; cleaned daily. *Beach facilities:* chalets for hire; cafe; toilets. *Dog restrictions:* "poop scoop" beach.

MARGATE

Family Fun Activities: Heated indoor leisure pool, indoor sports/leisure centre, amusement arcades • Shell Grotto, The Droit House, Margate Museum (contact VIC before visiting) • Lifeboat Station • Ten-pin bowling, bowls, indoor bowls, tennis, putting, pitch and putt, golf course, mini-golf, crazy golf, adventure golf, angling • Casino, theatres, nightclubs, disco, bandstand.

Kent

⭐ **Special Events: Feb/March:** Quad Bike Racing. **June:** Margate Big Event. **June/July:** Open Bowls Tournament, Volleyball Competition. **July:** Big Sky Jazz Festival. **August:** Carnival Parade. **September:** Kite Festival.

ℹ️ **Visitor Information Centre, 12-13 The Parade, Margate CT9 1EY
0870 264 6111
e-mail: tourism@thanet.gov.uk
www.visitthanet.co.uk**

🏖️ Beaches

- **MARGATE MAIN SANDS.** rejuvenated harbour area with cafes/bars; 200 metres long, sandy beach, promenade and boardwalk, parking, ♿ access. *Safety and maintenance:* warning flags, animal logo signposts to help children find their way back to parents, first-aid station, lifeguards and lifeboat; bay inspector/ information, beach cleaned daily. *Beach facilities:* sun loungers, deckchairs for hire; tidal boating pool, donkey rides; kiddies' corner; cafes, restaurants, pubs; toilets with ♿ access. *Dog restrictions:* not permitted on beach 1 May to 30 September incl.

- **PALM BAY/HODGES GAP & FORENESS POINT.** 200 metres long; sandy, sheltered beach, parking. *Safety and maintenance:* cleaned daily. *Beach facilities:* designated water-ski and jet ski area; toilets. *Dog restrictions:* "poop scoop" beach.

- **WALPOLE BAY.** Sandy beach 400 metres long, popular watersports bay, tidal pool, lift, promenade, parking, ♿ access. *Safety and maintenance:* warning flags, lifeguards; cleaned daily. *Beach facilities:* chalets and jet skis for hire; cafe, toilets. Monthly Farmers' Market. *Dog restrictions:* dog ban 1 May to 30 September incl.

- **WESTBROOK BAY.** 200 metres long, sandy; promenade and parking. *Safety and maintenance:* warning flags, lifeguards, bay inspector/information; first-aid station; cleaned daily. *Beach facilities:* deck chairs, chalets for hire; designated water ski area; adventure golf; cafe; toilets with ♿ access. *Dog restrictions:* banned from 1 May to 30 September 10am to 6pm.

RAMSGATE

🎪 **Family Fun Activities:** Heated indoor leisure pool, sports and leisure centre • Maritime Museum (contact VIC before visiting) • Royal harbour and yacht marina • Amusement arcades, leisure park and boating pool, tennis, bowls, angling • Theatre, cinema, discos.

⭐ **Special Events: June:** Great Bucket & Spade Run. **July:** Powerboat and Waterski Grand Prix, Carnival Parade, Costumed Walks. **August:** Open Bowls Tournament, International Sailing Week. **September:** Model Ships Rally.

ℹ️ **Visitor Information Centre, 17 Albert Court, York Street, Ramsgate CT11 9DN • 0870 264 6111
e-mail: tourism@thanet.gov.uk
www.visitthanet.co.uk**

🏖️ Beaches

- **MAIN SANDS.** Popular sandy beach, 250 metres long; promenade and parking, ♿ access. *Safety and maintenance:* animal logo signposts to help children find their way back to their parents, warning flags, lifeguards, bay inspector/information; first-aid station; beach cleaned daily. *Beach facilities:* donkey rides; deck chairs, sun loungers for hire; amusements, children's play area; cafes, restaurants, pubs, shops; toilets with ♿ access; Edwardian lift to beach. *Dog restrictions:* not permitted on beach 1 May to 30 September incl.

- **PEGWELL BAY.** A stretch of unprotected sea cliffs with great geological interest. Part of Kent's largest national Nature Reserve. Toilets, cafe, picnic area, parking.

Bolden's Wood
Fiddling Lane, Stowting, Near Ashford, Kent TN25 6AP

Between Ashford/Folkestone. Friendly atmosphere – modern accommodation (one double/twin, one single) on our Smallholding, set in unspoilt countryside. No smoking throughout. Full English breakfast. Country pubs (meals) nearby. Children love the old-fashioned farmyard, free range chickens, friendly sheep and... Llamas, Alpacas and Rheas. Treat yourself to a Llama-led Picnic Trek to our private secluded woodland and downland and enjoy watching the bird life, rabbits, foxes, badgers and occasionally deer.
Easy access to Channel Tunnel and Ferry Ports.
Bed and Breakfast £25.00 per person.   Contact: Jim and Alison Taylor

Tel & Fax: 01303 812011
e-mail: StayoverNight@aol.com
www.countrypicnics.com

☆ Fun for all the Family ☆

◆ **Canterbury Tales, Canterbury (01227 479227).** Chaucer's 14th century tales brought vividly to life by the latest audio-visual technology.
www.canterburytales.org.uk

◆ **Eagle Heights, Eynsford (01322 866577).** One of the UK's largest bird of prey centres with over 50 species of raptors. Daily flying demonstrations, and collection of reptiles and mammals.

◆ **Kent Life, near Maidstone (01622 763936).** Heritage farm attraction with 28 acres of fun for all generations, with animals, historic artefacts and regular special events.
www.kentmuseum.co.uk

◆ **Romney, Hythe and Dymchurch Railway (01797 362353).** Runs from Hythe to Dungeness – 13.5 mile journey through beautiful landscape.
www.rhdr.org.uk

◆ **South of England Rare Breeds Centre, Ashford (01233 861493).** Set in 120 acres of unspoilt countryside - friendly farm animals, indoor and outdoor play areas, Discovery Garden.
www.rarebreeds.org.uk

◆ **Wingham Bird Park, near Canterbury (01227 720836).** Set in 25 acres of beautiful countryside, with large walk-through aviaries, reptile house, adventure playground.

Garden of England Cottages

Accommodation for all seasons

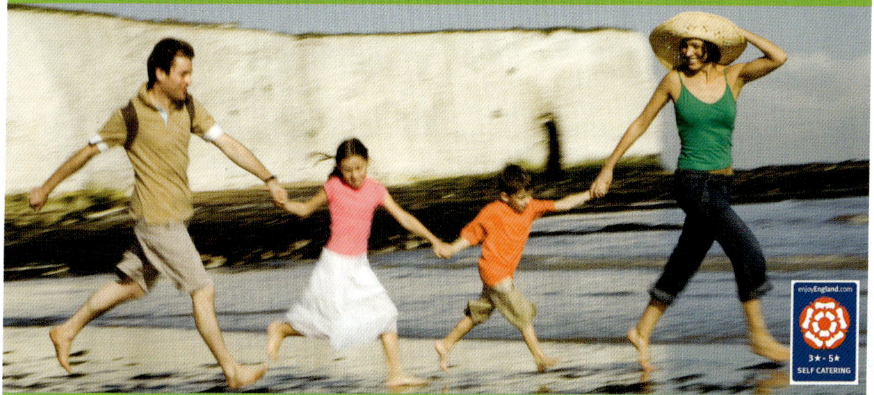

Allow our friendly locally based team to help you choose a holiday property for that feeling of total freedom and peace of mind.

ON-LINE BOOKING AND AVAILABILITY

info@gardenofenglandcottages.co.uk **Tel: +44 (0)1892 510117**

Bramley Knowle Farm B&B & Apple Pye Self-catering Cottage

★★★★ BED & BREAKFAST

enjoyEngland.com ★★★★ SELF CATERING

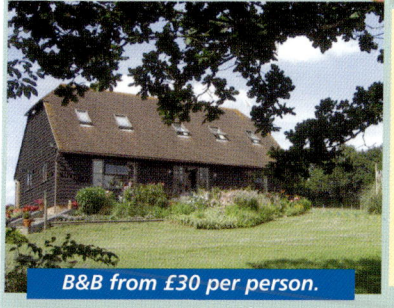

B&B from £30 per person.

A warm welcome awaits you at our modern farmhouse built in the style of a Kentish Barn, set in 45 acres of land surrounded by peaceful countryside. Only 10 minutes' drive from M20, J8, it is an ideal central location, close to Leeds Castle, Sissinghurst, Canterbury. London 1¼ hours by train, Dover one hour by car.

One double room en suite, one family suite (single/twin and double with shared bathroom), all with tea/coffee making facilities, TV, central heating, wireless broadband. Ample off-road parking.

Cottage on farm set in 45 acres, surrounded by beautiful rolling Kentish countryside. Well away from the road and next to the farmhouse B&B.

Sleeps four. One double room en suite, one twin with own shower room; living room/kitchen/dining room with washer/dryer, fridge/freezer, electric cooker, microwave, TV, DVD, wireless broadband. Full central heating. Garden and patio. Suitable for disabled.

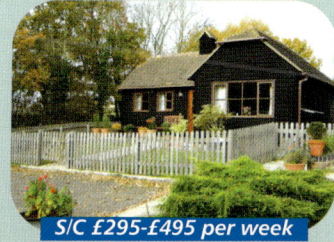

S/C £295-£495 per week

Mr & Mrs Leat, Bramley Knowle Farm, Eastwood Road, Ulcombe, Maidstone, Kent ME17 1ET
Tel: 01622 858878 • e-mail: diane@bramleyknowlefarm.co.uk • www.bramleyknowlefarm.co.uk

LONDON & HOME COUNTIES

[i] **Visit London**
1 Warwick Row, London SW1E 5ER
- Tel: 020 7932 2000
- Fax: 020 7932 0222
e-mail: enquiries@visitlondon.com
- www.visitlondon.com

HISTORIC BUILDINGS

◆ **Hampton Court, East Molesey, Surrey** (0844 482 7777). Built over 400 years ago, this became one of Henry VIII's royal palaces. Tudor tennis court, Great Vine and Maze. Nearest BR station: Hampton Court.
www.hrp.org.uk

◆ **Houses of Parliament and Strangers' Gallery**: if you wish to listen to a debate apply in advance to your MP or join the queue at St Stephen's Entrance on the day.
www.parliament.uk

◆ **Kensington Palace** (0844 482 7777). State Apartments of the late Stuart and Hanoverian periods containing 17th century furniture and pictures. Nearest Tube: Queensway.
www.hrp.org.uk

◆ **St Paul's Cathedral** (020 236 4128). Sir Christopher Wren's masterpiece built between 1675 and 1710. Nearest Tube: St Paul's, Mansion House.
www.stpauls.co.uk

◆ **Tower of London** (0844 482 7777). Built by William the Conqueror as a fortress, this magnificent building today houses the Crown Jewels. Nearest Tube: Tower Hill.
www.hrp.org.uk

◆ **Westminster Abbey** (020 7222 5152). Founded by Edward the Confessor in 1065, the Abbey has become the burial place of many famous people. Nearest Tube: Westminster.
www.westminster-abbey.org

MUSEUMS & GALLERIES

British Museum (020 7323 8299).
www.britishmuseum.org
Imperial War Museum (020 7416 5320).
www.iwm.org.uk
Museum of London (020 7814 5530).
www.museumoflondon.org.uk
National Gallery (020 7747 2885).
www.nationalgallery.org.uk
National Maritime Museum (020 8858 4422).
www.nmm.ac.uk
National Portrait Gallery (7306 0055).
www.npg.org.uk
Natural History Museum (020 7942 5000).
www.nhm.ac.uk
Royal Academy of Arts (020 7300 8000).
www.royalacademy.org.uk
Science Museum (0870 870 4868).
www.sciencemuseum.org.uk
Tate Britain (020 7887 8888).
www.tate.org.uk
Tate Modern (020 7887 8888).
www.tate.org.uk

London & Home Counties

◆ **V&A Museum of Childhood (020 8983 5200)**. A child's world of toys, dolls, dolls' houses, children's costumes.
www.vam.ac.uk

◆ **London Transport Museum (020 7379 6344)**. A collection of historic vehicles illustrating the development of London's transport system. Nearest Tube: Covent Garden.
www.ltmuseum.co.uk

VISITOR ATTRACTIONS

◆ **British Airways London Eye, South Bank, London (0870 5000 600)**. Stunning views over Central London and beyond during a half-hour ride on the gently moving 135m high observational wheel.
www.londoneye.com

◆ **Chessington World of Adventures (0870 999 0045)**. Exciting theme areas, rides, circus and zoo – a world of adventure for all the family. BR: Chessington South.
www.chessington.com

◆ **HMS Belfast (020 7940 6328)**. The last survivor of the Royal Navy's big ships, now a permanent floating museum. Nearest Tube: London Bridge.
http://hmsbelfast.iwm.org.uk

◆ **Kew Gardens, near Richmond (020 8332 5655)**. 300 acres, once belonging to the Royal family, now contains 25000 different plant species; greenhouses, herbarium and museums. Tube: Kew Gardens.
www.kew.org

◆ **Legoland, Windsor (0871 2222 001)**. A theme park with a difference, all set in 150 acres of wooded parkland.
www.legoland.co.uk

◆ **London Dungeon (020 7403 7221)**. The world's first medieval horror exhibition featuring gruesome scenes of torture, murder and depravation. Perfect for the kids! Nearest Tube: London Bridge.
www.thedungeons.com

◆ **London Zoo (020 7722 3333)**. One of the largest zoos in the world containing a varied collection of animals, birds, reptiles and insects. New Children's Zoo tells how people and animals live side by side. Nearest Tube: Camden Town.
www.zsl.org

◆ **Madame Tussaud's (0870 400 3000)**. The world famous waxworks of contemporary and historic figures complete with the inevitable Chamber of Horrors. Nearest Tube: Baker Street.
www.madametussauds.com

◆ **Royal Observatory, Greenwich (020 8858 4422)**. Includes Wren's Flamsteed House, Meridian Building and Planetarium. New high precision pendulum clock donated by Moscow Research Centre.
www.nmm.ac.uk

Big Ben with the London Eye in the background

London & Home Counties

Chase Lodge Hotel
An Award Winning Hotel
with style & elegance, set in tranquil surroundings at affordable prices.
10 Park Road Hampton Wick Kingston-Upon-Thames KT1 4AS Children Welcome
Tel: 020 8943 1862 . Fax: 020 8943 9363
e-mail: info@chaselodgehotel.com • www.chaselodgehotel.com

Quality en suite bedrooms
Close to Bushy Park
Buffet-style Full Continental Breakfast

Licensed bar
Wedding Receptions
Honeymoon suite
available with jacuzzi & steam area
20 minutes from Heathrow Airport
Close to Kingston town centre & all major transport links.

All Major Credit Cards Accepted

★★★

Barry House
12 Sussex Place, Hyde Park, London W2 2TP
- Comfortable, family-friendly B&B
- En suite, double, triple and family rooms
- Rates include English Breakfast
- Near Hyde Park and Oxford Street
- Paddington Station 4 minutes' walk

www.barryhouse.co.uk
hotel@barryhouse.co.uk
fax: 020 7723 9775

Call us now on: 0207 723 7340

We believe in family-like care

Ask for your Family Breaks discount

Elizabeth Hotel

Quiet, convenient townhouse overlooking the magnificent gardens of Eccleston Square. Only a short walk from Buckingham Palace and other tourist attractions. Easy access to Knightsbridge, Oxford Street and Regent Street.
Extremely reasonable rates in a fantastic location.

Visa, Mastercard, Maestro and Delta are all accepted.

37 Eccleston Square, Victoria, London SW1V 1PB

info@elizabethhotel.com
www.elizabethhotel.com
Tel: 020 7828 6812
Fax: 020 7828 6814

London & Home Counties

 # Queens Hotel

33 Anson Road, Tufnell Park, LONDON N7 0RB
Tel: 0207 607 4725; Fax: 0207 697 9725
E-Mail: queens@stavrouhotels.co.uk   www.stavrouhotels.co.uk

The Queens Hotel is a large double-fronted Victorian building standing in its own grounds five minutes' walk from Tufnell Park Station. Quietly situated with ample car parking spaces; 15 minutes to West End and close to London Zoo, Hampstead and Highgate. Two miles from King's Cross and St Pancras Stations. Many rooms en suite.

All prices include full English Breakfast plus VAT. Children at reduced prices. Discounts on longer stays

Stavrou Hotels is a family-run group of hotels.
We offer quality and convenience at affordable rates.
A VERY WARM WELCOME AWAITS YOU.

Single Rooms from £30-£55
Double/Twin Rooms from £40-£69
Triple & Family Rooms from £20 per person

Our hotels accept all major Credit cards, but some charges may apply.

London & Home Counties

Gower Hotel

129 SUSSEX GARDENS, HYDE PARK, LONDON W2 2RX
Tel: 0207 262 2262; Fax: 0207 262 2006
E-Mail: gower@stavrouhotels.co.uk   www.stavrouhotels.co.uk

The Gower Hotel is a small family-run Hotel, centrally located, within two minutes' walk from Paddington Station, which benefits from the Heathrow Express train "15 minutes to and from Heathrow Airport".

Excellently located for sightseeing London's famous sights and shops, Hyde Park, Madame Tussaud's, Oxford Street, Harrods, Marble Arch, Buckingham Palace and many more close by.

All rooms have private shower and WC, radio, TV (includes satellite and video channels), direct dial telephone and tea and coffee facilities. All recently refurbished and fully centrally heated. 24 hour reception.

All prices are inclusive of a large traditional English Breakfast & VAT

Discount available on 3 nights or more if you mention this advert

Stavrou Hotels is a family-run group of hotels.
We offer quality and convenience at affordable rates.
A VERY WARM WELCOME AWAITS YOU.

Single Rooms from £30-£79
Double/Twin Rooms from £60-£89
Triple & Family Rooms from £80

Our hotels accept all major Credit cards, but some charges may apply.

London & Home Counties

 # The Athena

110-114 SUSSEX GARDENS, HYDE PARK, LONDON W2 1UA
Tel: 0207 706 3866; Fax: 0207 262 6143
E-Mail: athena@stavrouhotels.co.uk   www.stavrouhotels.co.uk

TREAT YOURSELVES TO A QUALITY HOTEL AT AFFORDABLE PRICES

The Athena is a newly completed family run hotel in a restored Victorian building. Professionally designed, including a lift to all floors and exquisitely decorated, we offer our clientele the ambience and warm hospitality necessary for a relaxing and enjoyable stay. Ideally located in a beautiful tree-lined avenue, extremely well-positioned for sightseeing London's famous sights and shops; Hyde Park, Madame Tussaud's, Oxford Street, Marble Arch, Knightsbridge, Buckingham Palace and many more are all within walking distance.

Travel connections to all over London are excellent, with Paddington and Lancaster Gate Stations, Heathrow Express, A2 Airbus and buses minutes away.
Our tastefully decorated bedrooms have en suite bath/shower rooms, satellite colour TV, bedside telephones, tea/coffee making facilities. Hairdryers, trouser press, laundry and ironing facilities available on request. Car parking available.

Stavrou Hotels is a family-run group of hotels.
We offer quality and convenience at affordable rates.
A VERY WARM WELCOME AWAITS YOU.

Single Rooms from £50-£89
Double/Twin Rooms from £64-£99
Triple & Family Rooms from £25 per person
All prices include full English breakfast plus VAT.

Our hotels accept all major Credit cards, but some charges may apply.

EAST OF ENGLAND

 Best Beaches

A very impressive total of 13 beaches in this area were proud winners in 2009 of the European Blue Flag for beaches meeting the strictest of standards. Several beaches also were proud winners of a Quality Coast Award.

East of England Tourism
Bedfordshire, Cambridgeshire, Essex, Hertfordshire, Norfolk, Suffolk).
- Tel: 01284 727470
- Fax: 01284 706657
- e-mail: info@eet.org.uk
- www.visiteastofengland.com

BLUE FLAG BEACHES 2009
- *Dovercourt Bay*
- *Brightlingsea*
- *Clacton-on-Sea*
- *Southend*
  Shoebury Common
  Shoeburyness
  Three Shells
- *Cromer*
- *Mundesley*
- *Sea Palling*
- *Sheringham*
- *Lowestoft*
  North
  South of Pier
- *Felixstowe South*

For more information about holidaying in East Anglia see:
- www.visitbeds-luton.com
- www.midbeds.gov.uk
- www.bedford.gov.uk
- wwww.vistcambridge.org
- wwww.essex-sunshine-coast.org.uk
- www.realessex.co.uk
- wwww.hertfordshire.com
- wwww.visitnorfolk.co.uk
- www.northnorfolk.org
- wwww.visit-suffolk.org.uk
- www.visitsuffolkattractions.co.uk

Leighton Buzzard Railway, Bedfordshire

CLACTON-ON-SEA

Family Fun Activities: Fun-packed pier with rides, amusements, cafes and fishing (wheelchair accessible) • Leisure centre with swimming pool • Two theatres, cinema, bingo, night clubs • Clacton Factory Shopping Village.

[i] Tourist Information Centre, Town Hall, Station Road, Clacton-on-Sea CO15 1SE • 01255 686633
e-mail: clactontic@tendringdc.gov.uk
www.essex-sunshine-coast.org.uk

Beaches

• BEACH. Long sandy beach, gently sloping. *Beach facilities:* deck chairs, beach cafes; toilets. *Dog restrictions:* dogs banned on some beaches during main holiday season.

SOUTHEND

Family Fun Activities: Pier (longest pleasure pier in the world), Sea Life Adventure, Cliffs Pavilion, Adventure Island • Sailing, water ski-ing, windsurfing, motor boats, marine activity centre • Indoor swimming pools, skateboard park, tennis, bowls, golf, miniature golf, putting, children's playgrounds • Museums, planetarium, art gallery; theatres, nightclubs, discos • The Kursaal indoor entertainments centre

[i] Visitor Information Centre, Southend Pier, Western Esplanade, Southend-on-Sea SS1 1EE
01702 215120 • Fax: 01702 431449
www.visitsouthend.co.uk

East of England 93

Beaches

• BEACHES. 7 miles of sea and foreshore with sand and shingle beach, stretching from Shoeburyness to Chalkwell and Leigh; ample parking. *Safety and maintenance:* cleaned daily boards with information on bathing water quality. *Beach facilities:* paddling pool, activity frame, beach shower; cafes, restaurants; toilets. *Dog restrictions:* from 1st May to 30th September must be kept on a lead on promenade.

GREAT YARMOUTH

Family Fun Activities: Yesterday's World, Marina Leisure Centre, Hollywood Indoor Golf, Pleasure Beach, Sea Life Centre, House of Wax, Model Village, Joyland Fun Park, "Amazonia" The Jungle at the Winter gardens - children's adventure play.• Stock car racing, greyhound racing, horse racing, golf; putting, pitch and putt, outdoor bowls, ten-pin bowling, indoor karting • Marina, boating, fishing, sea cruises, Broads cruises, horse riding, indoor swimming pools, squash, tennis amusement arcades, children's playgrounds, Pirates' Cove (novelty golf), piers, road train • Museums, theatres, circus, cinema, nightclubs.

★ **Special Events:** Fireworks Displays, Herring Festival, Festival of Bowls, Maritime Festival. Carnivals and fêtes, band concerts.

[i] Tourist Information Centre, 25 Marine Parade, Great Yarmouth NR30 2EN • 01493 846346
e-mail: tourism@great-yarmouth.gov.uk
www.great-yarmouth.co.uk

FREE AND REDUCED RATE HOLIDAY VISITS!
Don't miss our Readers' Offer Vouchers on pages 163-180

Beaches

- **GREAT YARMOUTH BEACH.** Sandy beach, five miles long; two piers with entertainment. *Safety and maintenance:* warning flags, lifeguards; cleaned regularly. *Beach facilities:* deck chairs, windbreaks, beach huts; trampolines, donkey rides, inflatables, horse drawn landaus, pleasure boat trips; ice-cream kiosks, snack bars, restaurants and pubs; toilets on sea front with ♿ access. *Dog restrictions:* banned from beach during main season.

- **GORLESTON BEACH.** One and a half miles long, sandy; promenade and pier with good parking adjacent. *Safety and maintenance:* warning flags, lifeguards; beach cleaned during summer season. *Beach facilities:* deck chairs, trampolines, beach huts and chalets; ice-cream kiosks, snack bars, restaurants and pubs; toilets with ♿ access. *Dog restrictions:* banned from Blue Flag section during main summer months.

LOWESTOFT

Family Fun Activities: Mayhem soft play area, museums, pier; swimming pool, indoor football centre, adventure golf, golf, putting, pitch and putt, tennis, bowling, horse riding, water sports, parks with children's playgrounds • Theatres, cinemas, discos, nightclubs. Nearby: New Pleasurewood Hills, Suffolk Wildlife Park, Transport Museum, Lowestoft Ness (Britain's most easterly point).

i **Tourist Information Centre, East Point Pavilion, Royal Plain, Lowestoft NR33 0AP • 01502 533600 e-mail: touristinfo@waveney.gov.uk www.visit-lowestoft.co.uk Brochure info line: 0870 6061303**

Beaches

- **KESSINGLAND BEACH.** Pebble and shingle with some sand; low cliffs, easy access. *Safety and maintenance:* cleaned by Local Authority. *Dog restrictions:* banned from 1st May to 30th September; must be kept on lead on promenade.

- **PAKEFIELD BEACH.** Sandy beach with some shingle below low grassy cliffs; parking. *Safety and maintenance:* cleaned by Local Authority; dangerous to clamber or swim near groynes. *Beach facilities:* pubs; toilets with ♿ access.

- **LOWESTOFT RESORT BEACHES.** Sandy pleasure beaches with two piers; esplanade and ample parking. *Safety and maintenance:* warning flags, lifeguards; dangerous to clamber or swim near groynes; cleaned daily. *Beach facilities:* children's corner, chalets, ice-cream kiosks, restaurants, snack bars, pubs; toilets with ♿ access. *Dog restrictions:* banned from 1st May to 30th September; must be kept on lead on promenade.

- **SOUTHWOLD RESORT BEACH.** Part sand, part shingle with sand dunes; refurbished pier including amusements and refreshments. Parking. *Safety and maintenance:* warning flags, lifeguards; cleaned by Local Authority. *Beach facilities:* beach huts; cafes, pubs; toilets. *Dog restrictions:* banned from 1st May to 30th September; must be kept on lead on promenade.

- **SOUTHWOLD DENES.** Part sand, part shingle with sand dunes. This rural beach is secluded and peaceful, an ideal place for walkers and nature enthusiasts. Parking. *Safety and maintenance:* cleaned by Local Authority.

www.holidayguides.com

East of England 95

★ Fun for all the Family ★

BEDFORDSHIRE

◆ **Whipsnade Wild Animal Park, Dunstable (01582 872171).** Britain's largest conservation centre specialising in breeding certain endangered species. Children's zoo, steam railway.
www.zsl.org

◆ **Woburn Safari Park (01525 290333).** Britain's largest drive-through safari park. Roundabouts and rides.
www.woburn.co.uk

CAMBRIDGESHIRE

◆ **Nene Valley Railway, Peterborough (01780 784444).** A preserved steam railway with 7½ miles of track. Cafe shop, museum and engine shed.
www.nvr.org.uk

◆ **Sacrewell Farm and Country Centre, Thornaugh (01780 782254).** 500-acre farm with working watermill, nature trails, displays of farming bygones.
www.sacrewell.org.uk

ESSEX

◆ **Colchester Zoo, Colchester (01206 331292).** World-wide collection of animals and birds, with daily displays of parrots, sealions and falcons. Penguin parade, snake handling, meet the elephants.
www.colchester-zoo.co.uk

HERTFORDSHIRE

◆ **Paradise Wildlife Park, Broxbourne (01992 470490).** 17 acres with lots of animals; woodland railway, adventure playgrounds, pony rides, aviary, education centre.
www.pwpark.com

NORFOLK

◆ **Banham Zoo, Banham (01953 887771).** Over 25 acres of wildlife in parkland setting with extensive collection of rare and endangered species. Road train, adventure playground and World of Penguins.
www.banhamzoo.co.uk

◆ **Dinosaur Adventure (01603 876310).** Walk through woodland to view dinosaurs in natural settings. Adventure rides, play area, wooded maze; bygones museum.
www.dinosauradventure.co.uk

◆ **Sea Life Centre, Great Yarmouth (0871 4232110).** A spectacular way to experience the underwater world, with themed tanks on local marine life.
www.sealife.co.uk

SUFFOLK

◆ **Easton Farm Park, Wickham Market (01728 746475).** Victorian farm setting for many species of farm animals including rare breeds. Nature trail, pets paddock and adventure playground.
www.eastonfarmpark.co.uk

◆ **Pleasurewood Hills Theme Park, Lowestoft (01502 586000).** Live shows and all the rides your family can handle! Off A12 between Great Yarmouth and Lowestoft.
www.pleasurewoodhills.co.uk

◆ **Africa Alive! Kessingland (01502 740291).** Suffolk's "walking safari" set in 100 acres of dramatic coastal parkland. Daily feeding sessions, safari road train, adventure playground.
www.africa-alive.co.uk

East of England

THE MEADOW HOUSE
2a High Street, Burwell,
Cambridge CB5 0HB
Tel: 01638 741926
Fax: 01638 741861

e-mail: hilary@themeadowhouse.co.uk

The Meadow House is a magnificent modern house set in two acres of wooded grounds offering superior Bed and Breakfast accommodation in spacious rooms, some with king-size beds. The variety of en suite accommodation endeavours to cater for all requirements; a suite of rooms sleeping six complete with south-facing balcony; a triple room on the ground floor with three single beds and the Coach House, a spacious annexe with one double and one single bed; also one double and two twins sharing a well equipped bathroom. All rooms have TV, central heating and tea/coffee facilities. Car parking. No smoking
Family rate available on request.

www.themeadowhouse.co.uk

High House Farm
Cransford, Framlingham, Woodbridge IP13 9PD
Tel: 01728 663461
e-mail: b&b@highhousefarm.co.uk
www.highhousefarm.co.uk

Exposed oak beams • inglenook fireplaces • one double room, en suite and one large family room with double and twin beds and private adjacent bathroom • children's cots • high chairs • books • toys • outside play equipment • attractive semi-moated gardens • farm and woodland walks.

Explore the heart of rural Suffolk, local vineyards, Easton Farm Park, Framlingham and Orford Castles, Parham Air Museum, Saxtead Windmill, Minsmere, Snape Maltings, Woodland Trust and the Heritage Coast.
Bed and Breakfast from £30. Reductions for children.

White Lodge Farm, Hingham, Norfolk NR9 4LY
Call 01953 850435 or 07768 156680
e-mail: fhgfb@whitelodgefarmcottages.co.uk
www.whitelodgefarmcottages.co.uk

East of England

Take a Blue Riband Holiday in beautiful Norfolk and take a pet free*

*One pet stays free when you book through this advert. Extra pet £10

Inexpensive Self Catering Holidays at ●Caister ●Hemsby ●Scratby ●Winterton ●California and ●Great Yarmouth **All year round**

Detached Bungalows at Parklands
Hemsby Village, Children's Playground, Digital Freeview TV, Miniature Railway.

Seafront Bungalows
Caister-on-Sea, with enclosed rear gardens leading to the beach.

Detached Chalets on Sea-Dell Park
Quiet location, Beach Road, Hemsby.

Belle Aire Park, Beach Rd, Hemsby
Premier Chalets. Free satellite TV. Clubhouse and safe children's playground. Pets are allowed on local beaches.
All equipped to very high standard
★ *Free car parking at all locations*
Open Christmas & New Year

Quality, Value and Service from a family business, since 1955

● **Popular low season breaks, bungalows from only £90**
● **Bargain Spring & Autumn breaks, excellent value chalets from £75**

☎ **Direct Line for Bookings & Brochures**
01493 730445 – Call 8am to 9pm 7 days a week
Debit / Credit Cards Accepted

Or browse our full brochure on our website at: www.BlueRibandHolidays.co.uk

For your free colour brochure phone the above number or write to:
Don Witheridge, Blue Riband House, Parklands, North Road, Hemsby, Great Yarmouth, Norfolk NR29 4HA

East of England

CASTAWAYS HOLIDAY PARK

Set in the quiet, peaceful village of Bacton, with direct access to fine sandy beach, and ideal for beach fishing and discovering Norfolk and The Broads. Modern Caravans, pine lodges and flats with all amenities • Licensed Club • Entertainment. Amusement Arcade • Children's Play Area • Pets welcome

on-line booking facility available Enquiries and Bookings to:

Castaways Holiday Park, Paston Road, Bacton-on-Sea NR12 0JB
Tel: 01692 650436/650418 • www.castawaysholidaypark.co.uk

Kessingland Cottage — Rider Haggard Lane, Kessingland

• Sleeps 6 • Children and disabled persons welcome • Available 1st March to 7th January •

An exciting three-bedroomed semi-detached cottage situated on the beach, three miles south of sandy beach at Lowestoft. Fully and attractively furnished with colour TV. Delightful sea and lawn views from floor-to-ceiling windows of lounge. Accommodation for up to six people. Well-equipped kitchen with electric cooker, fridge, hot and cold water; electric immersion heater. Electricity by £1 coin meter. Bathroom with bath and shower. No linen or towels provided. Only a few yards to beach and sea fishing. One mile to wildlife country park with mini-train. Buses quarter-of-a-mile and shopping centre half-a-mile. Parking, but car not essential.

SAE to Mr. S. Mahmood, 156 Bromley Road, Beckenham, Kent BR3 6PG (Tel & Fax: 020 8650 0539)
e-mail: jeeptrek@kjti.co.uk • www.k-cottage.co.uk

Weekly terms from £95 in early March and early December to £375 in high season.

Beach Farm Residential & Holiday Park Ltd

1 Arbor Lane, Pakefield, Lowestoft, Suffolk NR33 7BD
Tel: 01502 572794 • Mobile: 07795 001449
e-mail: beachfarmpark@aol.com • www.beachfarmpark.co.uk

A friendly, peaceful family-run park set in six acres of attractive, sheltered surroundings only 500 yards from Pakefield beach and supermarket, 2 miles from the town centre.

- De luxe caravan holiday homes with central heating
- Deluxe Country Lodges (3-bed)
- Luxury residential Park homes for sale
- Limited spaces for touring / camping inc. hook-ups
- Licensed bar / beer garden with children's play area
- Seasonal entertainment
- Outdoor heated swimming pool
- Launderette • Restaurant adjacent

The park is very close to many local attractions including Pleasurewood Hills Theme Park and Africa Alive.

Midlands 99

MIDLANDS

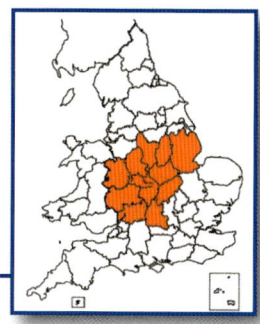

 Best Beaches

Four beaches in the East Midlands area have attained the standards necessary to have won a Blue Flag for 2009.

BLUE FLAG BEACHES 2009
- Mablethorpe
- Cleethorpes Central
- Skegness
- Sutton on Sea

i **East Midlands Tourism**
(Leicestershire & Rutland, Lincolnshire, Northamptonshire, Nottinghamshire, Peak District & Derbyshire).

www.enjoyenglandseastmidlands.com

For other counties in the Midlands see individual Tourist Boards (below)

FREE AND REDUCED RATE HOLIDAY VISITS!
Don't miss our
Readers' Offer Vouchers
on pages 163-180

For more information about holidaying in the Midlands see:
- www.glos-cotswolds.com
- www.visitherefordshire.co.uk
- www.shropshiretourism.info
- www.enjoystaffordshire.com
- www.visitnorthernwarwickshire.com
- www.visitshakespeare-country.co.uk
- www.worcestershire-tourism.org

Heritage Motor Centre, Warwickshire

Midlands

☆ Fun for all the Family ☆

DERBYSHIRE

◆ **Gulliver's Kingdom, Matlock Bath. (01925 444888).** Theme park set in 15 acres of wooded hillside, designed especially for younger children.
www.gulliversfun.co.uk

◆ **Heights of Abraham, Matlock Bath. (01629 582365).** Spectacular cable car ride to hilltop country park. Show caverns, visitor centre, restaurant.
www.heightsofabraham.com

◆ **Crich Tramway Village, Crich (01773 854321).** Tramcars from all over the world; scenic displays, restaurant, children's playground.
www.tramway.co.uk

GLOUCESTERSHIRE

◆ **National Waterways Museum, Gloucester (01452 318200).** Recreates the story of Britain's inland waterways. Working machinery, demonstrations.
www.nwm.org.uk

◆ **Slimbridge Wetland Centre, Slimbridge (01453 891900).** Over 2300 birds of 180 different species, including in winter wild swans, geese and ducks. Activities throughout the year.
www.wwt.org.uk

◆ **Sudeley Castle, Winchcombe. (01242 602308).** Toys, treasures, peacock gardens, children's play area. Katherine Parr (Henry VIII's Queen) buried here.
www.sudeleycastle.co.uk

LEICESTERSHIRE

◆ **Moira Furnace & Craft Workshops, Near Ashby de la Zouch (01283 224667).** Impressive 19th century blast furnace museum. Woodland walks, nature trail, children's play area.
www.moirafurnace.com

◆ **Snibston Discovery Park, Coalville. (01530 278444).** Exhibition hall with 5 galleries exploring the county's industrial heritage, plus outdoor science play area, colliery tours.
www.leics.gov.uk/museums/snibston

LINCOLNSHIRE

◆ **Natureland Seal Sanctuary, Skegness (01754 764345).** Entertainment, education and conservation: baby seals, penguins, free-flight tropical birds, plus lots of other fascinating creatures.
www.skegnessnatureland.co.uk

◆ **National Fishing Heritage Centre, Grimsby (01472 323345).** Tells the story of fishermen, their boats and the waters they fished in; the dangers and hardships of life at sea are explained.
www.nelincs.gov.uk

NOTTINGHAMSHIRE

◆ **Sherwood Forest Country Park and Visitor Centre, Near Mansfield (0844 980 8080).** Includes visitor centre with Robin Hood Exhibition, guided walks, picnic sites, and refreshments.
www.nottinghamshire.gov.uk

FREE or REDUCED RATE entry to Holiday Visits and Attractions
see our **READERS' OFFER VOUCHERS** on pages 163-180

☆ Fun for all the Family ☆

OXFORDSHIRE

◆ **Blenheim Palace, Woodstock (08700 602080)**. Home of the Duke of Marlborough, with magnificent collection of tapestries and porcelain. Landscaped grounds with butterfly house, adventure playground and railway. World Heritage Site.
www.blenheimpalace.com

◆ **Cotswold Wild Life Park, Burford (01993 823006)**. A large and varied collection of animals from all over the world in natural surroundings.
www.cotswoldwildlifepark.co.uk

SHROPSHIRE

◆ **Ironbridge Gorge Museum, Telford (01952 884391)**. Award-winning museum complex which brings industrial history to life. Working museums and real history - the images and objects of the industrial revolution.
www.ironbridge.org.uk

◆ **Hoo Farm Animal Kingdom, near Telford (01952 677917)**. Friendly llamas, inquisitive ostriches, plus lots more. Undercover and outdoor attractions.
www.hoofarm.com

STAFFORDSHIRE

◆ **Alton Towers, Alton (08705 204060)**. Europe's premier leisure park – rides, gardens, monorail, shops, adventure play areas etc.
www.altontowers.com

◆ **Drayton Manor Theme Park, Near Tamworth (0844 472 1950)**. Over 100 heart stopping range of rides, including Apocalypse, Shockwave and Stormforce 10; nature trail, zoo, parkland and lakes.
www.draytonmanor.co.uk

WARWICKSHIRE

◆ **Heritage Motor Centre, Gaydon (01926 641188)**. Purpose-built transport museum containing collection of historic British cars. Site includes four-wheel drive circuit.
www.heritage-motor-centre.co.uk

◆ **The Shakespearian Properties, Stratford-upon-Avon (01789 868191)**. Five distinctive homes including Shakespeare's Birthplace and Anne Hathaway's Cottage, all administered by the Shakespeare Birthplace Trust.
www.stratford-upon-avon.co.uk

◆ **Warwick Castle, Warwick (0870 442 2000)**. Britain's greatest medieval experience – castle with dungeon, armoury and torture chamber, all set in 60 acres of grounds.
www.warwick-castle.co.uk

WEST MIDLANDS

◆ **National Sea Life Centre, Birmingham (0871 423 2110)**. Bringing the magic of the marine world to the heart of Birmingham with over 55 displays of marine and freshwater creatures. Features the world's first 360° fully transparent viewing tunnel.
www.sealife.co.uk

◆ **Thinktank at Millennium Point, Birmingham (0121 202 2222)**. 10 themed galleries where you can examine the past, investigate the present, and explore what the future may bring.
www.thinktank.ac

WORCESTERSHIRE

◆ **West Midland Safari Park, Bewdley (01299 402114)**. 4-mile drive-through safari, live shows and attractions. From reptiles to roller coasters – it's all here!
www.wmsp.co.uk

DOG & PARTRIDGE
· COUNTRY INN ·

Mary and Martin Stelfox welcome you to a family-run 17th century Inn and Motel set in five acres, five miles from Alton Towers and close to Dovedale and Ashbourne. We specialise in family breaks, and special diets and vegetarians are catered for. All rooms have private bathrooms, colour TV, direct-dial telephone, tea-making facilities and baby listening service.

Ideal for touring Stoke Potteries, Derbyshire Dales and Staffordshire Moorlands. Open Christmas and New Year.

'Staffs Good Food Winners 2003/2004'.

Restaurant open all day, non-residents welcome

e-mail: info@dogandpartridge.co.uk
Tel: 01335 343183 • www.dogandpartridge.co.uk
Swinscoe, Ashbourne DE6 2HS

Tel: 01298 23875 • www.devarms.com

Traditional inn in the heart of the Peak District.
Close to all main attractions.
Excellent walking country.

- All rooms refurbished to a high standard.
- En suite, TV, tea/coffee facilities.
- Excellent meals and traditional ales
- Children's menu.
- Warm welcome to all.
- Dogs free.
- Prices from £32.50

The Devonshire Arms
Peak Forest, Near Buxton, Derbyshire SK17 8EJ

Midlands

THE Old Stocks
Hotel, Restaurant & Bar
The Square, Stow-on-the-Wold GL54 1AF

Ideal base for touring this beautiful area. En suite family rooms. Full English breakfasts included. Extensive lunch and dinner menu. Large three-terraced patio garden and own car park.

Budget; Christmas and New Year Breaks available.

Tel: 01451 830666
Fax: 01451 870014
e-mail: fhg@oldstockshotel.co.uk
www.oldstockshotel.co.uk

AA ★★ SMALL HOTEL

SMALL HOTEL

Linhill Guest House
35 Evesham Place,
Stratford-upon-Avon CV37 6HT
Tel: 01789 292879
e-mail: linhill@bigwig.net
www.linhillguesthouse.co.uk

Linhill is a comfortable Victorian Guest House run by a friendly family. It is situated only five minutes' walk from Stratford's town centre with its wide choice of fine restaurants and world famous Royal Shakespeare Theatre. Every bedroom at Linhill has central heating, colour TV, tea/coffee making facilities and washbasin. En suite facilities are also available, as are packed lunches and evening meals. Bicycle hire and babysitting facilities if desired. Leave the children with us and re-discover the delight of a candlelit dinner in one of Stratford's inviting restaurants.

Midlands   105

Alison Park Hotel

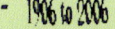

Situated close to the Pavilion Gardens and within a few minutes' walk of the Opera House.
- 17 bedrooms, all with either en suite or private bathroom.
- Full English or Continental breakfast, full dinner menu and an extensive wine list; lunches, bar meals and dinner available daily.
- Vegetarian and special diets catered for.
- Lounge with colour TV.
- All bedrooms have tea & coffee makers, colour TV etc.
- Wheelchair ramp access. • Ground floor bedrooms.
- Lift to all floors. • Conference facilities. • Licensed.

There are many stately homes and gardens to visit in the area including Chatsworth, Haddon Hall, and Lyme Park – location for *"Pride and Prejudice."* Alton Towers is less than an hour's drive away; Gulliver's Kingdom, for younger children, and the cable car at the Heights of Abraham only 30 minutes by car. .Almost every kind of outdoor pursuit can be enjoyed in the Peak District from potholing and rock climbing to hang gliding. Walking or cycling the many beautiful tracks, trails and pathways of Derbyshire is very popular. Cycle hire is widely available.

ALISON PARK HOTEL
3 Temple Road, Buxton SK17 9BA
Tel: 01298 22473 • Fax: 01298 72709
e-mail: reservations@alison-park-hotel.co.uk
www.alison-park-hotel.co.uk

Situated in Staffordshire Moorlands, cosy 3 bedroomed cottage (sleeps 6), overlooking picturesque countryside. Fully equipped, comfortably furnished and carpeted throughout. Cottage, all on ground floor and with three bedrooms (one with four-poster). An ideal base for visits to Alton Towers, the Potteries and Peak District. Patio, play area. Cot and high chair available. Laundry room with auto washer and dryer. Electricity and fresh linen inclusive. Terms from £230 to £375.

EDITH & ALWYN MYCOCK
'ROSEWOOD COTTAGE'
LOWER BERKHAMSYTCH FARM, BOTTOM HOUSE, NEAR LEEK ST13 7QP
Tel & Fax: 01538 308213
www.rosewoodcottage.co.uk

Rochford Park Cottages

Tenbury Wells WR15 8SP • Tel & Fax: 01584 781392
e-mail: cottages@rochfordpark.co.uk

Located on one of the Teme Valley's working farms, this former dairy (sleeps 3) and barn (sleeps 8) are now stylish, comfortable retreats for any holidaymaker.

Explore the farm's footpaths and bridleways, fish in one of its lakes, play golf on the neighbouring 9-hole links....
Further afield, walk the Malvern Hills, or valleys of the Welsh Marches.

Hereford, Worcester and Ludlow are within 30 miles as are numerous National Trust and English Heritage houses and gardens.

Youngsters will enjoy the Severn Valley Railway and Bewdley Safari Park. Open all year round.
For further details see our website.

www.rochfordpark.co.uk

Woodland Hills Court
Holiday Cottages

We have 5 brick built holiday cottages. Four have two double/ twin bedrooms, one of which is wheelchair-friendly. The fifth cottage has one bedroom with a 4-poster bed and a bathroom with a roll-topped bath.

All five cottages have an open-plan, well equipped kitchen, dining room and lounge with colour TV and DVD player.

The four two-bedroom cottages have a modern, good-sized wet room. There are gardens and patios for each cottage for added privacy, and full use of a drying and laundry room for our guests.

- All linen and towels are provided.
- A child's cot is available on request.
- Electricity is extra, each cottage having its own meter.
- There is ample off road parking.

South Derbyshire offers lots of entertainment for all ages, Donington Park motor racing, Alton Towers, Calke Abbey, Kedleston Hall, Twycross Zoo, and lots more in the new National Forest, including horse riding.

A starter pack will be placed in your cottage; flowers and/or chocolates arranged on request.

Price from £350 to £500 per week
Short stays subject to availability, priced at £250 for a 4 night stay.

**Woodland Hills Court
Ivy House Farm
Stanton by Bridge
Derby DE73 7HT
Tel: 01332 863152
info@ivy-house-farm.com
www.woodlandhillscourt.co.uk**

Stratford-upon-Avon

RIVERSIDE LOCATION – ONLY ONE MILE FROM THE TOWN CENTRE

LUXURY HOLIDAY HOMES FOR HIRE • TOURING CARAVANS AND MOTORHOME PITCHES • RIVERFRONT COTTAGES TO RENT

Short Stay Bookings Welcome & 3-day Long Weekend Deals

Set in the heart of the lovely Warwickshire countryside and right on the banks of the beautiful River Avon, is Riverside Caravan Park, the perfect location for exploring Shakespeare Country and the Cotswolds. Holiday Home units accommodate 6 persons and Riverford Cottages 4 persons comfortably.

RIVER TAXIS TO AND FROM TOWN • ADJACENT LOCAL VILLAGE • FREE FISHING • RIVERSIDE WALKS ON SITE SHOP & CAFE • CLUB HOUSE • KIDS PLAYGROUND

Riverside Caravan Park

Tiddington Road
Stratford-upon-Avon
Warwickshire CV37 7AB

01789 292312

www.stratfordcaravans.co.uk

A small touring park, very clean and quiet, set in the countryside two miles south west of Stratford-upon-Avon. An ideal location from which to visit Shakespeare's birthplace, Anne Hathaway's Cottage, Warwick Castle and the Cotswolds. There are country walks to the River Avon and the village of Luddington. From Stratford-upon-Avon take B439 (formerly A439) towards Bidford-on-Avon for two miles. The park lies on the left, signposted. Free brochure on request.
From £14.50 to £19.00 including electricity • Open all year.
Over 50 years as a family business

A warm welcome awaits!

Dodwell Park is very well equipped to make your camping stay homely and comfortable. These are some of our facilities: -
Toilets • Free hot showers • Washhand basins with hot water
Hand and hair dryers • Shaving points
Calor and Camping Gaz • Dishwashing facilities
Shop and off-licence • Hard standings • Electric hook-ups
Public telephone and post box • Dogs are welcome

**Evesham Road (B439)
Stratford-upon-Avon
Warwickshire
CV37 9SR**

Tel: 01789 204957
enquiries@dodwellpark.co.uk
www.dodwellpark.co.uk

NORTH-EAST ENGLAND

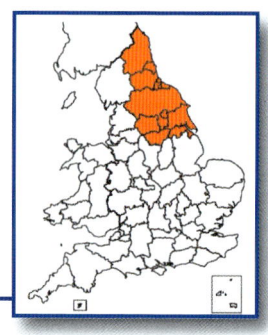

 **Best Beaches**

This year no less than 9 beaches on this impressive stretch of coastline have won a European Blue Flag. Several beaches have also gained a Quality Coast Award.

ℹ️ **North East England Tourism**
- **Tel: 01904 707961**
- **Fax: 01904 707070**
- **www.visitnortheastengland.com**

Blue Flag Beaches 2009
- *Tynemouth*
  King Edward's Bay
  Longsands South
- *Roker*
- *South Shields, Sandhaven*
- *Whitby West Cliff*
- *Scarborough North Bay*
- *Bridlington North*
- *Hornsea*
- *Whitley Bay South*

For more information about holidaying in the North East see:
www.visitteesvalley.co.uk
www.visitnorthumberland.com
www.visitcountydurham.com
www.visitnewcastlegasteshead.co.uk

National Railway Museum, York

BRIDLINGTON

Family Fun Activities: Summer shows • Children's attractions • Sports and games, golf, boating, fishing, wind-surfing • Indoor Leisure World (4 pools). New: Eye of the Bay (big wheel)

Special Events: May: Week-long festival of street and theatre shows. **August:** Lions Carnival. **September:** Sea angling week. **October:** Carnival Championships.

Information Centre, 25 Prince Street, Bridlington YO15 2NP
Tel: 01262 673474
www.realyorkshire.co.uk

Beaches

- **NORTH BEACH.** Two miles long, sandy and naturally sheltered, with cliffs and rock pools towards northern end. Promenade; good parking. *Safety and maintenance:* cleaned daily. *Beach facilities:* deck chairs; various entertainments on beach; ice cream kiosks, snack bars, restaurants and pubs; toilets with ♿ access. *Dog restrictions:* banned May to end September, must be kept on lead on Promenade.

- **SOUTH BEACH.** Two miles long, sandy and naturally sheltered with some dunes at southern end. Promenade and good parking. *Safety and maintenance:* cleaned daily. *Beach facilities:* deck chairs; beach chalets for hire; beach activities; donkey rides; ice cream kiosks, snack bars, restaurants and pubs; toilets with ♿ access (open 24 hours in summer). *Dog restrictions:* banned May to end September, must be kept on lead on Promenade.

CLEETHORPES

Family Fun Activities: Leisure Centre, Pleasure Island Theme Park, Cleethorpes Coast Light Railway, Discovery Centre, The Jungle Zoo; 10-Pin Bowling Centre, Promenade Gardens, Lakeside Sand Pit and Paddling Pool, Fantasy World; Laser Adventure • Crazy golf, amusement arcades, children's entertainment, night clubs, discos.

Special Events: May: Kite Festival. **July/August:** Carnival Week and Parade. Markets: Wednesday and Sunday.

Tourist Information Centre, Cleethorpes Library, Alexandra Road, Cleethorpes DN35 8LG
Tel: 01472 323111 • Fax: 01472 323112
e-mail: cleetic@nelincs.gov.uk
www.enjoycleethorpes.com

Beaches

- **NORTH PROMENADE.** Sandy and naturally sheltered; promenade; good parking. *Safety and maintenance:* Beach Safety Officers; sandbanks; beach cleaned daily. *Beach facilities:* deck chairs; donkeys, swings, Big Wheel, fairground; ice cream kiosks, snack bars, restaurants, pubs; toilets with ♿ ramps. *Dog restrictions:* from 1st April to 30th September dogs are restricted on various clearly marked areas of the beach.

- **CENTRAL PROMENADE.** Three-quarters of a mile long, sandy; naturally sheltered Promenade and good parking. *Safety and maintenance:* cleaned daily; Beach Safety Officers, warning signs. *Beach facilities:* deck chairs; donkeys, horses and carts, land train; ice cream kiosks, snack bars, pubs; toilets with ♿ ramps. *Dog restrictions:* from April 1st to 30th September dogs are restricted on various clearly marked areas of the beach.

FILEY

Family Fun Activities: Boating lake, putting, crazy golf, trampolines, children's play area, miniature golf • Bird Garden & Animal Park, Folk Museum, Filey Dams Nature Reserve, Filey Brigg Nature Trail, Filey Sculpture Trail.

☆ Special Events: June/July: Filey Festival. **July:** Filey Regatta. **August:** Life Boat Day. **August/September:** Fishing Festival.

Tourist Information Centre, John Street, Filey YO14 9DW
01723 383637 • Fax: 01723 518001
www.discoveryorkshirecoast.com

Beaches

• **BEACH.** Miles of open sand, naturally sheltered; parking. *Safety and maintenance:* cleaned daily, flagged, warning signs; lifeguards. *Beach facilities:* deckchairs, beach chalets; donkey rides; cafe and ice-cream kiosk; toilets with ♿ access. *Dog restrictions:* banned between Coble Landing and Royal Parade (seasonal).

SCARBOROUGH

Family Fun Activities: Heated indoor pool, spa, sports centre, crown green bowls, 10-pin bowling, tennis, putting, two golf courses • Mini railway, boating lake, angling in harbour • Amusement arcades, bingo, cinemas, theatre, nightclubs • Museums and 12thC castle • Bird of Prey Centre, Shire Horse Farm, mini "naval warfare", Sea Life Centre, Honey Farm, Terror Tower, pleasure boat trips, Dino Days (Dinosaur Coast events).

Tourist Information Centre, Sandside, Scarborough YO11 1PP
01723 383637 • Fax: 01723 383604
tourismbureau@scarborough.gov.uk
www.discoveryorkshirecoast.com

☆ Special Events: May/June: Scarborough Fayre; festivals, International Music Festival. **July:** Seafest. **September:** Jazz Festival.

Beaches

• **NORTH BAY BEACH.** Three-quarters of a mile long, sandy with rockpools and cliffs. Promenade, good parking. *Safety and maintenance:* cleaned daily; flagged, warning signs, lifeguards. *Beach facilities:* deck chairs and beach chalets; donkey rides; putting and boating lake. *Dog restrictions:* 1st May to 30th September - no dogs permitted between Scalby Mills and mini roundabout; must be kept on lead on Promenade.

• **SOUTH BAY BEACH.** Half a mile long, sandy and naturally sheltered. Promenade, bay includes Scarborough harbour with three piers. Good parking. *Safety and maintenance:* cleaned daily; flagged, warning signs, lifeguards. *Beach facilities:* deck chairs and beach chalets; donkey rides; swings and roundabouts; toilets with ♿ access. *Dog restrictions:* 1st May to 30th September - no dogs permitted from West Pier to Spa Footbridge.

Scarborough Bay

North East 113

WHITBY

Family Fun Activities: Heated indoor pool, boating, yachting, trout and salmon fishing, putting, crazy golf, golf,; bowls • Leisure Centre • Theatres, pavilion, museum, art gallery • Remains of 11th century abbey, Dracula Experience Trail, Captain Cook Heritage Trail, Funtastic indoor play area.

Special Events: March: Eskdale Festival of Arts. **August:** Whitby Regatta.

Tourist Information Centre,
Langborne Road, Whitby YO21 1YN
01723 383637 • Fax: 01947 606137
tourismbureau@scarborough.gov.uk
www.discoveryorkshirecoast.com

Beaches

• **BEACH.** Three miles long, sandy and naturally sheltered. Good parking. *Safety and maintenance:* cleaned daily; warning signs, lifeguards. *Beach facilities:* deck chairs and beach chalets; donkey rides; ice cream kiosk and snack bar; toilets with ♿ access. *Dog restrictions:* May to September – banned between Battery Parade and former Beach Cafe; must be kept on lead on Battery Parade and Promenade.

FREE AND REDUCED RATE HOLIDAY VISITS!
Don't miss our Readers' Offer Vouchers on pages 163-180

☆ Fun for all the Family ☆

COUNTY DURHAM

◆ **The Josephine and John Bowes Museum, Barnard Castle (01833 690606).** Outstanding art collection, plus ceramics, porcelain, tapestries, and objects d'art (including Silver Swan automaton).
www.bowesmuseum.org.uk

◆ **Beamish, The North of England Open Air Museum, Beamish (0191 370 4000).** A vivid re-creation of how people lived and worked at the turn of the century. Town Street, Home Farm, Colliery, Railway Station; tram rides, tea rooms.
www.beamish.org.uk

EAST YORKSHIRE

◆ **Elsham Hall Country and Wildlife Park, Near Brigg (01652 688698).** See working craftsmen demonstrate their traditional skills in the craft centre set in beautiful grounds and lakeside gardens. Children's farm, lake, adventure playground, falconry centre.
www.elshamhall.co.uk

◆ **The Deep, Hull (01482 381000).** Discover the story of the world's oceans on a dramatic journey back in time and into the future! The world's only underwater lift and Europe's deepest viewing tunnel!
www.thedeep.co.uk

NORTHUMBERLAND

◆ **Alnwick Castle (01665 510777).** A mighty fortress, seat of the Duke of Northumberland since 1309. Location for the 'Harry Potter' films.
www.alnwickcastle.com

◆ **Grace Darling Museum, Bamburgh (01668 214465).** Many original relics re-create the rescue by Grace and her father of the survivors of the wrecked Forfarshire.

◆ **Leaplish Waterside Park, Kielder Water (01434 220643).** Ideal base for exploring the largest man-made lake in Britain; all sorts of sports, forest playground, restaurant.
www.kielder.org

★ Fun for all the Family ★

TEES VALLEY

◆ **Captain Cook Birthplace Museum, Middlesbrough (01642 311211).** Special effects add realism to the museum displays which tell the story of the famous explorer.
www.captcook-ne.co.uk

◆ **Hartlepool Historic Quay, Hartlepool (01429 860077).** Travel back in time to the sights, sounds and smells of 18th century seaport life. New attractions include children's adventure playship.
www.thisishartlepool.co.uk

TYNE & WEAR

◆ **Life Science Centre, Newcastle-upon-Tyne (0191 243 8210).** Discover just how truly amazing life is. Explore where life comes from and how it works. Meet your 4 billion year old family, find out what makes you unique, test your brainpower and enjoy the thrill of the Motion Simulator Ride.
www.life.org.uk

◆ **Wildfowl and Wetlands Trust, Washington (0191-416 5454).** Have a great day out supporting conservation on a nose-to-beak voyage of discovery – many birds feed from the hand. Exhibition area, tea room, play area.
www.wwt.org.uk

NORTH & WEST YORKSHIRE

◆ **Eden Camp Modern History Theme Museum, Malton (01653 697777).** Civilian life in Britain during WWII – experience the sights, sounds and even smells of 1939-1945 at this award-winning museum.
www.edencamp.co.uk

◆ **Flamingo Land Theme Park, Zoo and Holiday Village, near Malton (0871 911 8000).** Rides and slides, zoo, indoor playcentre, cable car ride etc.
www.flamingoland.co.uk

◆ **Lightwater Valley Theme Park, Ripon (0871 720 0011).** The world's longest roller coaster, thrill rides, theatre, crazy golf, boating lake and much more. Restaurant and cafes.
www.lightwatervalley.co.uk

◆ **National Media Museum, Bradford (0870 701 0200).** Packed with things to do and find out, this bright, modern museum is a fun day out for all the family, telling the fascinating story of still and moving pictures.
www.nationalmediamuseum.org.uk

◆ **National Railway Museum, York (08448 153139).** See how Britain's railways shaped the world at the largest railway museum in the world. BR's up to-the-minute exhibit gives a glimpse into the future. Restaurant and gift shop.
www.nrm.org.uk

◆ **Royal Armouries Museum, Leeds (08700 344344).** Thousands of items from a collection previously housed in the Tower of London. Jousting displays, Oriental swordsmanship, plus lots more.
www.armouries.org.uk

Please note

All the information in this book is given in good faith in the belief that it is correct. However, the publishers cannot guarantee the facts given in these pages, neither are they responsible for changes in policy, ownership or terms that may take place after the date of going to press. Readers should always satisfy themselves that the facilities they require are available and that the terms, if quoted, still apply.

North East

Orillia House
89 The Village, Stockton on Forest, York YO32 9UP

A warm welcome awaits you at Orillia House, conveniently situated in the centre of the village, three miles north east of York, one mile from A64. The house dates back to the 17th century and has been restored to offer a high standard of comfort with modern facilities yet retaining its original charm and character. All rooms have private facilities, colour TV and tea/coffee making facilities. Our local pub provides excellent evening meals. We also have our own private car park. Telephone for our brochure

B&B from £25pppn sharing double room.

Tel: 01904 400600
e-mail: info@orilliahouse.co.uk
www.orilliahouse.co.uk

GUEST ACCOMMODATION ★★★★

Witton Castle
COUNTRY PARK County Durham

Set within the castle grounds among 338 acres of some of the North's finest and most beautiful countryside, Witton Castle Country Park is fast becoming the number one place to own your own holiday home.

Phase one of the most ambitious project underway in the north east is virtually complete, and with high demand from both first time buyers and people who already have holiday homes and are looking for the best, we now have very limited pitches available on Castle View - so if you're thinking about investing in a holiday home somewhere a bit special, phone for a guided tour now - or just call in. Close to home but a world away.

See you soon!

WANTED
- Reasonable site fees ✓
- Wide, 5 star pitches ✓
- Block paved driveways, paths & patios ✓
- Piped gas ✓
- Bar & restaurant ✓
- Over 21s bar ✓
- Children's room ✓
- Expansive grounds ✓
- Children's playground ✓
- Football & outdoor games ✓
- Walking & cycling routes ✓
- No tents or rentals ✓
- Easy access from home ✓
- A country estate not just a caravan park ✓
- A castle? ✓

DO YOU OWN YOUR OWN CARAVAN?
DON'T PAY YOUR SITE FEES UNTIL YOU'VE SEEN THE RE-DEVELOPED **WITTON CASTLE**
2010 SITE FEES **FROZEN AGAIN**

For a FREE information pack please visit:
www.wittoncastlecountrypark.co.uk
or call us on: **01388 488 230**

For Sat Navs, use:
'Sloshes Lane' and 'DL14 0DE'

Witton Castle Country Park, Sloshes Lane, Nr Witton-Le-Wear, County Durham, DL14 0DE

North East

Set in the tiny hamlet of Greenhouses and enjoying splendid views over open countryside, three cottages offering a very quiet and peaceful setting for a holiday. The cottages have been converted from the traditional farm buildings and the olde world character has been retained in the thick stone walls, exposed beams and red pantile roofs. All are well equipped, and linen, fuel and lighting are included in the price. There are ample safe areas for children to play.

Sorry, no pets. Prices from £295 to £645 per week. Winter Breaks from £200.

Foxglove Cottage for 3 persons
Two bedrooms - one double, one single. Lounge, dining kitchen, shower room and separate toilet.

Honeysuckle Cottage for 6 persons
Four bedrooms - two double and two single. Lounge, dining/ kitchen. One bathroom with toilet. One shower room with washhand basin and toilet.

Primrose Cottage for 4 persons
Two bedrooms - one twin downstairs. One double upstairs. Open plan lounge, dining kitchen. Bathroom with toilet. Suitable for the disabled.

**Nick Eddleston, Greenhouses Farm Cottages, Greenhouses Farm, Lealholm, Near Whitby N. Yorkshire YO21 2AD
01947 897486**

www.greenhouses-farm-cottages.co.uk

Other specialised holiday guides from FHG

PUBS & INNS OF BRITAIN
COUNTRY HOTELS OF BRITAIN
WEEKEND & SHORT BREAKS IN BRITAIN & IRELAND
THE GOLF GUIDE WHERE TO PLAY, WHERE TO STAY
PETS WELCOME!
500 GREAT PLACES TO STAY IN BRITAIN
BED & BREAKFAST STOPS IN BRITAIN
CARAVAN & CAMPING HOLIDAYS IN BRITAIN
SELF-CATERING HOLIDAYS IN BRITAIN

Published annually: available in all good bookshops or direct from the publisher:
FHG Guides, Abbey Mill Business Centre, Seedhill, Paisley PA1 1TJ
Tel: 0141 887 0428 • Fax: 0141 889 7204
e-mail: admin@fhguides.co.uk • www.holidayguides.com

Rudding Park

Relax with your family
in the heart of Yorkshire...

Self Catering Cottages and Chalet Lodges in beautiful surroundings

Spacious 5 star Luxury Lodges

Generous sized Camping & Caravanning pitches

- Deer House family pub
- Children's adventure playground
- Pets welcome in most properties
- Heated outdoor swimming pool and paddling pool
- 18 hole Pay and Play golf course plus floodlit driving range
- Six hole short course
- Games room

Rudding Park, Follifoot, Harrogate, North Yorkshire HG3 1JH
T: **01423 871350** | E: **reservations@ruddingpark.com**
www.ruddingpark.co.uk

NORTH WEST ENGLAND

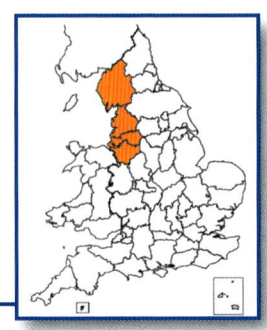

Best Beaches

There are lovely stretches of coastline and clean sands, and lively resorts whose efforts to maintain their high place in British holiday planning are showing successful results. Blackpool South Beach, St Anne's Pier, Ainsdale, Crosby and Sefton have each earned a Quality Coast Award.

 **North West Tourism**
(Cheshire, Greater Manchester, High Peak, Lancashire, Merseyside).
- **www.englandsnorthwest.com**

For more information about holidaying in the North West see:
- www.visitlancashire.com
- www.visitchester.com
- www.golakes.co.uk
- www.visitliverpool.com
- www.visitmanchester.com

St Anne's Pier, Lancashire

FREE AND REDUCED RATE HOLIDAY VISITS!
Don't miss our
Readers' Offer Vouchers
on pages 163-180

North West

BLACKPOOL

Family Fun Activities: Pleasure Beach with over 145 rides and attractions including Europe's tallest, fastest rollercoaster and Valhalla, the world's biggest dark ride • Blackpool Tower with 7 levels of fun including a circus, ballroom, adventure playground and aquarium • Zoo, Sealife Centre, Sandcastle Waterworld indoor water paradise, Louis Tussaud's Waxworks • Stanley Park with lake, Italian Gardens, bowling, children's playgrounds, putting and Sports Centre • Three piers with arcades, shows and amusements, Winter Gardens with ballroom and Opera House, Grand Theatre • 10-pin bowling, golf, putting, go-karts, fishing, swimming pools • Multiplex cinemas, shows, pubs.

Special Events: July/August: Kids MegaFest Children's Festival. **1st September to 5th November:** Blackpool Illuminations.

i Blackpool Tourism, 1 Clifton Street, Blackpool FYl lLY • 01253 478222
e-mail: tourism@blackpool.gov.uk
www.visitblackpool.com

Beaches

• **BEACH.** Approximately 7 miles long, sandy. Promenade, tramcars; good parking. *Safety and maintenance:* foreshore flagged, warning signs; lifeguards; beach cleaned daily. *Beach facilities:* deck chairs, donkey rides; ice cream kiosks, snack bars, restaurants, pubs; toilets with special needs access and mother/baby changing facilities. *Dog restrictions:* banned from the beach between North Pier and South Pier from May to September; must be kept on a lead on every street in Blackpool.

LYTHAM ST ANNES

Family Fun Activities: Pier, donkey rides on beach; children's playground, boating lake, floral gardens; tennis, putting, bowls, trampolines; miniature railway; golf courses (4); sailing; pubs, cafes and restaurants; theatre at Lytham; RSPB Discovery Centre at Fairhaven Lake.

Special Events: May/August: Carnivals and Fete days, miscellaneous local shows and competitions throughout the year.

i Visitor and Travel Information, Lytham St Annes FY8 ILW
01253 725610 • Fax: 01253 640708

Beaches

• **BEACH.** Sandy, three miles long, and backed by dunes and promenade. Pier with arcade and refreshments. Good parking. *Safety and maintenance:* patches of soft sand and mud; river estuary; warning signs. Cleaned daily in season. *Beach facilities:* deck chairs, donkey rides; ice cream kiosks, snack bars, restaurants; toilets with ♿ access. *Dog restrictions:* can be exercised north of St. Annes pier, past the high water mark.

Blackpool Illuminations

MORECAMBE

Family Fun Activities: Happy Mount Park (including Splash Park), Superbowl, Megazone and Cinema • Promenade and play areas, Stone Jetty with seabird-themed pavement games, arcades and amusements.
See our family-fun page:
www.citycoastcountryside.co.uk/site/what-to-see-and-do/family-fun

Special Events: Free family events include: **July:** Catch the Wind Kite Festival. **August:** Sandcastle Festival. **September:** "We do like to be beside the seaside".

Morecambe Visitor Information Centre, Old Station Buildings, Marine Road Central, Morecambe LA4 4DB
01524 582808 • Fax: 01524 832549
e-mail: morecambetic@lancaster.gov.uk
www.citycoastcountryside.co.uk

Beaches

• **BEACH.** Several stretches of sand, backed by 5 mile long flat promenade with beautiful views across the wide expanse of Morecambe Bay towards the Lake District. Ample parking. *Safety and maintenance:* safety signs and lifebelts; Promenade Supervisor. *Beach facilities:* ice cream kiosks; toilets incl. some with ♿ access; miniature train. *Dog restrictions:* dogs not allowed on amenity beaches.

BRITAIN'S BEST BEACHES
See pages 8-11

☆ Fun for all the Family ☆

CHESHIRE

◆ **Blue Planet Aquarium, Ellesmere Port (0151 357 8804).** The UK's largest aquarium with moving walkway through tropical fish and a large collection of sharks.
www.blueplanetaquarium.com

◆ **Boat Museum, Ellesmere Port (0151-355 5017).** World's largest floating collection of canal craft on a 7-acre site. Steam engines, blacksmith's forge etc. Cafe.
www.boatmuseum.org.uk

◆ **Catalyst, Widnes (0151-420 1121).** Science and technology comes alive with hands-on exhibits, observatory. The only science centre solely devoted to chemistry, with over 100 different exhibits.
www.catalyst.org.uk

◆ **Chester Zoo, Chester (01244 380280).** Britain's largest zoo in the UK. Spacious enclosures. Restaurants and cafeteria.
www.chesterzoo.org.uk

◆ **Jodrell Bank Science Centre, Planetarium and Arboretum, Near Macclesfield (01477 571339).** 'Hands on' gallery and space exhibition; planetarium. Lovell Radio Telescope.
www.jb.man.ac.uk

◆ **Stapeley Water Gardens, Nantwich (01270 623868).** Something for the whole family. Children will enjoy the Palms Tropical Oasis which includes a rainforest with unusual inhabitants.
www.stapeleywg.com

North West

★ Fun for all the Family ★

CUMBRIA

◆ **Cars of the Stars Motor Museum, Keswick (017687 73757).** Celebrity TV and film vehicles including Chitty Chitty Bang Bang and the Batmobile plus film set displays.
www.carsofthestars.com

◆ **The Bond Museum, Keswick (017687 74044).** 007 memorabilia, including original cars and props, including Aston Martins and the Dragon Tank from Dr No.
www.thebondmuseum.com

◆ **The Cumberland Pencil Museum, Southey Works, Keswick (01900 609599).** The first-ever pencils were produced in Keswick and the museum traces the history of this everyday writing instrument. See the longest pencil in the world.
www.pencils.co.uk

◆ **Eden Ostrich World, Penrith (01768 881771).** See these magnificent birds in the setting of a real farm on the banks of the River Eden. Play areas, farm animals.
www.ostrich-world.com

◆ **Lake District National Park Visitor Centre, Brockhole, Windermere (01539 724555).** Exciting Lake District exhibitions, including the 'Living Lakeland' display. Restaurant and tearooms.
www.lake-district.gov.uk

◆ **Rheged Centre, Penrith (01768 868000).** Journey through 2000 years of Cumbria's magic in this new attraction set under a grass-covered roof. Discover the village in the hill.
www.rheged.com

GREATER MANCHESTER

◆ **The Lowry, Salford (0870 787 5780).** A world-class venue for performing and visual arts. Theatres and galleries.
www.thelowry.com

◆ **Museum of Science and Industry, Manchester (0161-832 2244).** Like no other museum you've ever been in. Xperiment! – interactive science centre; Power Hall; Victorian Sewers – and lots more.
www.mosi.org.uk

LANCASHIRE

◆ **Blackpool Tower (01253 622242).** 520 ft high, houses a circus, aquarium, dance hall and other shows. The famous Illuminations start early in September.
www.theblackpooltower.co.uk

◆ **Wildfowl Trust, Martin Mere (01704 895181).** Exotic and native breeds plus thousands of migrant visitors observed from spacious hides.
www.wwt.org.uk

MERSEYSIDE

◆ **The Beatles Story, Liverpool (0151-709 1963).** Re-live the sights and sounds of the Swinging Sixties a magical mystery tour!
www.beatlesstory.com

◆ **World of Glass, St Helens (01744 22766).** The fascinating history of glass-making. Enter the magical mirror maze and explore the cone building tunnels.
www.worldofglass.com

North West

Families are welcome at this Regency Country House set in its own grounds in the heart of the Lake District, just ¼ mile from Lake Windermere and a short walk from the centre of Ambleside. Personally managed by the Nixon family for over 40 years, it still retains the comfortable, relaxed atmosphere of a private house and is well known for the friendly ambience and excellent cuisine. The hotel has 16 bedrooms (including 6 family rooms) and 3 family suites, 2 of which are in the grounds.

ROTHAY MANOR
HOTEL & RESTAURANT

Guests have free use of a nearby Leisure Club with children's pool, sauna, steam room and jacuzzi.

**Children's High Tea
Cots
High Chairs
Baby listening**

AA ★★★ One Red Rosette • ★★★ VisitBritain • Silver Award
*Good Food Guide for over 40 years • Cumbria for Excellence Small Hotel of the Year 2006
Short listed for Cumbria Tourism "Taste" Awards 2008*
**Rothay Bridge, Ambleside, Cumbria LA22 0EH • Tel: 015394 33605
e-mail: hotel@rothaymanor.co.uk • www.rothaymanor.co.uk**

Rakefoot Farm
Chaigley, Near Clitheroe BB7 3LY
VisitBritain ★★★★
VisitBritain ★★★/★★★★
Tel: (Chipping) 01995 61332 or 07889 279063 • Fax: 01995 61296
e-mail: info@rakefootfarm.co.uk • www.rakefootfarm.co.uk
Family farm in the beautiful countryside of the Ribble Valley in the peaceful Forest of Bowland, with panoramic views. Ideally placed for touring Coast, Dales and Lakes. 9 miles M6 Junction 31a. Superb walks, golf and horse riding nearby, or visit pretty villages and factory shops. Warm welcome whether on holiday or business, refreshments on arrival.
BED AND BREAKFAST or SELF-CATERING in 17th century farmhouse and traditional stone barn conversion. Wood-burning stoves, central heating, exposed beams and stonework. Most bedrooms en suite, some ground floor. Excellent home cooked meals service, pubs/restaurants nearby. Garden and patios. Dogs by arrangement. Laundry.

**B&B £25 - £35pppn sharing, £25 - £40pn single
S/C four properties (3 can be internally interlinked)
£111 - £695 per property per week. Short breaks available.**

*Fun for all the family at
The World of Glass,
St Helens, Lancs*

THE CHADWICK HOTEL

A Hotel for All Seasons

South Promenade, Lytham St Annes FY8 1NP

In all seasons, the Chadwick Hotel will meet and exceed your expectations, ensuring it won't be long before you want to return.

It is situated yards from the sandy beach, with panoramic views across the Ribble Estuary and Irish Sea, in the heart of Lytham St Annes and Lancashire. The hustle and bustle of Blackpool is minutes away and the picturesque Lake District within an hour, making it the perfect spot for a family holiday or short getaway. There is a lovely promenade and beach walks, a wide variety of shopping - and Lytham St Annes is a golfer's dream.

Open throughout the year whatever the weather, the hotel provides amenities to help you relax and enjoy your stay, from leisure facilities including the Atlantis pool, jacuzzi, sauna, Turkish bath, solarium and cardio gym, to the games room and soft play area for younger guests.

The hotel has 75 comfortably appointed rooms, with all modern conveniences. There are family rooms (with baby listening), singles and ground floor rooms for easy access, all en suite.

The Four Seasons Restaurant offers traditional and modern cuisine in a relaxed atmosphere. Children's portions are available, or the 'Little Seasiders' menu offers a selection for their discerning tastes.

The Bugatti Bar offers lighter meals, with an extensive list of wines and beers. 24-hour lounge and room service is available.

Why not try our themed and speciality weekends for something a little different, with the entertainment, food and 'feel' of faraway places? All the family will feel at home, and to us every occasion is a special one.

Tel: 01253 720061
www.thechadwickhotel.com
sales@thechadwickhotel.com

Low Wood Hotel ★★★★
LAKE WINDERMERE

This lakeshore hotel offers an excellent range of leisure and conference facilities. There is a selection of 110 bedrooms, many of them boasting fantastic, panoramic views across Lake Windermere.

All bedrooms are attractively furnished offering all the comfort and luxury you would expect for a truly memorable stay. There are a choice of bars, a contemporary and spacious restaurant and the more informal Bistro, Café del Lago. There is an exclusive Leisure Club, Beauty Salon and Watersports Centre onsite at the hotel offering a range of activities for everyone to enjoy.

Low Wood, Lake Windermere, Cumbria LA23 1LP
Reservations: 08458 503 502
website: www.elh.co.uk • e-mail: lowwood@elhmail.co.uk

North West

GREEN GABLES
37 Broad Street, Windermere LA23 2AB

A family-owned and run licensed guesthouse in Windermere centrally situated one-minute's walk from village centre with shops, banks and pubs and only five minutes from the station or bus stop. Accommodation comprises two doubles, one family triple/twin and one single room, all en suite; one family (four) and two family triple/twin rooms with private facilities; all with central heating, colour TV, hairdryers, kettles, tea & coffee. Comfortable lounge bar on the ground floor. No smoking in bedrooms. We can book tours and trips for guests and can advise on activities and special interests. B&B from £23 to £30 pppn. Special Winter offers available.
Open just about all year round.
Contact **Carole Vernon and Alex Tchumak**.

Tel: 015394 43886
e-mail: greengables@FSBdial.co.uk
e-mail: info@greengablesguesthouse.co.uk

Outgate, Ambleside LA22 0NH
Contact: Mr Evans • 015394 36583

Six timber lodges of varied size and design set in 15 acres of mixed woodland with wild flowers, birds and native wild animals. There are also 11 acres of rough hill pasture. Three miles south west of Ambleside, it is an ideal centre for walkers, artists, birdwatchers, and country lovers.

No pets • Children welcome • Open March to November

Ramsteads Coppice

North West

Stay Lakeland

Offering a range of high quality, pet friendly self catering holiday accommodations in the Lake District & Cumbria, including Traditional Cottages, Houses, Timber Lodges and Holiday Static Caravans. All our properties are graded at a ★★★ minimum and are inspected annually by VisitBritain.

Visit our website:
www.StayLakeland.co.uk
for easy online booking or call us on
0845 468 0936

Skiddaw View Holiday Home Park

here's the view...

Tel: 016973 20919
www.SkiddawView.co.uk

Skiddaw View is an award winning holiday home park, situated in a secluded and delightful setting on the outskirts of Bassenthwaite in the Northern Lake District. The twenty acre park is nestled into the hillside with panoramic views of Skiddaw and the Northern Fells. We can offer a range of self catering holiday properties including holiday static caravans, timber lodges as well as a number of holiday cottages in the surrounding towns and villages.

Bothel, near Bassenthwaite, Cumbria, CA7 2JN

North West

Greenhowe Caravan Park
Great Langdale, English Lakeland

Greenhowe Caravan Park
Great Langdale, Ambleside,
Cumbria LA22 9JU

Greenhowe is a permanent Caravan Park with Self Contained Holiday Accommodation. Subject to availability Holiday Homes may be rented for short or long periods from 1st March until mid-November. The Park is situated in the Lake District half-a-mile from Dungeon Ghyll at the foot of the Langdale Pikes. It is an ideal centre for Climbing, Fell Walking, Riding, Swimming. **Please ask about Short Breaks.**

LODGES also available

For free colour brochure
Tel: (015394) 37231 • Fax: (015394) 37464
www.greenhowe.com

Jenkin Cottage

Come and enjoy a peaceful away from it all holiday at our family-run working hill farm three miles from Cockermouth. Jenkin Cottage has a spectacular outlook over open countryside with views extending to the Solway Firth and the Scottish Lowlands. We are in an ideal situation for fell walking on the Buttermere fells or for touring the Lakes by car. The cottage is personally supervised and has a homely atmosphere. We are open all year with long weekends and mid week breaks in the winter months.

♦ All linen provided ♦ Lounge with open log fire ♦ Fully equipped modern kitchen ♦ Full central heating ♦ Sorry, no pets ♦ Children welcome ♦ We also extend a welcome to business people ♦ Terms from £250 to £500 per week ♦ Brochure available.

Mrs M.E. Teasdale, Jenkin Farm and Cottage, Embleton, Cockermouth CA13 9TN
Tel: 017687 76387 • e-mail: jenkin@sheepsnest.demon.co.uk • **www.jenkinfarm.co.uk**

Fisherground Farm
Eskdale, Cumbria

Fisherground is a lovely traditional hill farm, with a stone cottage and 3 pine lodges, sharing an acre of orchard.
Ideal for walkers, nature lovers, dogs and children, we offer space, freedom, peace and tranquillity.
We have a games room, a raft pool and an adventure playground.
Good pubs nearby serve excellent bar meals.
Ian & Jennifer Hall, Orchard House, Applethwaite, Keswick, Cumbria CA12 4PN
Tel: 017687 73175
holidays@fisherground.co.uk
www.fisherground.co.uk

North West

Cottages in and around Hawkshead, "the prettiest village in the Lake District".

Romantic cosy cottages to large houses for that special family gathering.

• open fires • pets welcome • free fishing • online booking

Tel: 015394 42435
www.lakeland-hideaways.co.uk

Lakeland Hideaways, The Square, Hawkshead LA22 0NZ

Whicham Hall Farm

A truly wonderful location, this single sited modern, static caravan enjoys unspoilt views of the beautiful Whicham Valley. Situated on a working beef/sheep farm at the foot of Backcombe mountain, with plenty of fell and beach walking on our doorstep. The caravan sleeps 4 people in two separate bedrooms, bedding provided. Gas cooking, electric heating and lighting, fridge, microwave and spin dryer. Shower room with basin, w.c. and shaver point. Sorry, no dogs. Children welcome. Ample parking. Terms from £200 to £350 per week. Short breaks out of season.

Mrs Capstick
Whicham Hall Farm, Whicham Valley, Silecroft, Cumbria LA18 5LT

Tel: 01229 772637 / 718112 • Mobile: 07974 367496

SCOTLAND

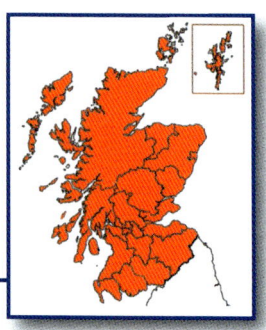

Best Beaches

Scotland has a huge coastline, one of the longest in Europe, with great stretches of sand along the Solway, on the Ayrshire coast, East Lothian and Fife, around Aberdeen, along the Moray Firth and in the North West. Good beach management practices have been rewarded with six European Blue Flags. In addition Seaside Awards (Resort and Rural Categories) have gone to beaches which meet the high standards required.

BLUE FLAG BEACHES 2009
- **St Andrews West Sands**
- **Aberdour Silver Sands**
- **Elie (Woodhaven)**
- **Broughty Ferry**
- **Burntisland**
- **Montrose**

Scottish Tourist Board
- Tel: 0845 2255 121
- e-mail: info@visitscotland.com
- www.visitscotland.com

Aberdeen Beach

Craigievar Castle, near Alford

Scotland

ABERDEEN

Family Fun Activities: Winter Gardens, Art Gallery, museums, cinemas, theatres, Music Hall • Doonies Farm, Hazlehead Park, Aberdeen Fun Beach, Satrosphere Hands-on Science Centre, Storybook Glen • Windsurfing, bowling, squash, tennis, cricket, rugby, riding, walking, climbing, fishing, golf.

Aberdeen Visitor Information Centre,
23 Union Street, Aberdeen AB11 5BP
01224 288828
Aberdeen.Information@visitscotland.com
www.visit-scotland.com

Beaches

• BEACH. Two and a half miles of sandy beach, promenade and harbour; ample parking. *Safety and maintenance:* cleaned daily; lifeboats, lifebelts; lifeguards in summer.
Aberdeen Fun Beach: Scotland's largest family entertainment centre, open all year. Restaurants, multi-plex cinema, leisure centre with swimming pool and flumes, ice arena, indoor and outdoor funfair, ten-pin bowling, pool and Ramboland – children's adventure play area

ISLE OF ARRAN

Family Fun Activities: This peaceful island, "Scotland in Miniature", offers a wealth of leisure activities and places of interest including Brodick Castle, Gardens and Country Park, Isle of Arran Distillery, Balmichael Visitor Centre, Isle of Arran Heritage Museum, Arran Aromatics.

Tourist Information Centre,
The Pier, Brodick KA27 8AU
0845 2255 121
e-mail: Brodick@visitscotland.com
www.ayrshire-arran.com

Special Events: **July:** Arran Fleadh. **August:** Highland Games. **October:** Ladies Golf Competition. **November:** Gents Golf Competition.

Beaches

• BEACHES. Varied coastline with shingle and pebble shores and sandy beaches suitable for all the family.

AYR

Family Fun Activities: Citadel Leisure Complex • Swimming pool, 10-pin bowling, golf, putting, pitch and putt, cricket, tennis, bowls • Cinema, dancing/discos • Racecourse • Nearby Burns National Heritage Park, Belleisle Park, Rozelle Park, Craig Tara, Heads of Ayr Park.

Special Events: **May:** Ayr Agricultural Show. **June:** Ayr Golf Week. **August:** Flower Show. **September:** Ayr Gold Cup (horse racing).

Tourist Information Centre,
22 Sandgate, Ayr KA7 1BW
0845 2255 121
e-mail: Ayr@visitscotland.com
www.ayrshire-arran.com

Beaches

• BEACH. Two and a half miles long, sand and some shingle; promenade and harbour; ample parking. *Beach facilities:* children's playground, crazy golf, boating pond, putting on promenade; cafes; toilets with ♿ access.

www.holidayguides.com

GIRVAN

Family Fun Activities: Swimming pool, golf, putting, tennis, bowls • Boat trips and fishing.

Special Events: **May:** Folk Festival. **June:** Civic Week. **August:** Annual Maidens Harbour Gala. **October:** Folk Festival.

Beaches

- **BEACH.** One and a half miles long, sandy and some shingle; promenade and harbour, ample parking. *Beach facilities:* children's playground, boating pond; toilets with ♿ access.

LARGS

Family Fun Activities: Swimming pool, sauna/solarium; tennis, putting, squash, golf, bowling, windsurfing, diving. • Vikingar, Kelburn Castle & Country Centre

Special Events: **August:** Regatta Week. **September:** Viking Festival.

Tourist Information Centre,
The Station, Largs
0845 2255 121
e-mail: Largs@visitscotland.com
www.ayrshire-arran.com

Beaches

- **BEACH.** Shingle and sand; promenade, parking; boating pond; cafes and ice cream kiosks; toilets with ♿ access.

MILLPORT

Family Fun Activities: Organised children's activities • Tennis, pitch and putt, trampolines, golf, riding, cycle hire, bowling, fun fair • Museum, aquarium at Marine Station • The Cathedral of the Isles (smallest cathedral in Britain). Millport is reached by car/passenger ferry from Largs; 10 minute bus ride from ferry slip to town.

Special Events: **July/August:** Country and Western Festival, Cumbrae Weekend.

Beaches

- **BEACH.** Sand and shingle, rock pools; parking. *Beach facilities:* cafes and shops nearby, toilets, some with ♿ access. *Dog restrictions:* must be kept on lead.

TROON

Family Fun Activities: golf, bowling, tennis, swimming, children's play areas.

Special Events: **June:** Gala Week.

www.ayrshire-arran.com

Beaches

- **BEACH.** Excellent sandy beach with first-aid and life saving equipment nearby. Toilets.

Looking for holiday accommodation?
search for details of properties where children are welcome
www.holidayguides.com

Scotland

ROTHESAY

Family Fun Activities: Main town on the Isle of Bute easily reached by car/passenger ferry from Wemyss Bay or Colintraive • Pavilion with family variety shows, children's entertainment • Mount Stuart, Isle of Bute Discovery Centre and cinema/theatre, Rothesay Castle, Bute Museum • Putting, tennis, bowling, golf, pony trekking • Leisure Pool with sauna/solarium • Ornamental gardens, castle and museum, walks.

i Isle of Bute Discovery Centre,
Victoria Street, Rothesay,
Isle of Bute PA20 0AH
0845 2255 121
e-mail: Rothesay@visitscotland.com
www.VisitBute.com

BRITAIN'S BEST BEACHES
See pages 8-11

ST ANDREWS

Family Fun Activities: Historic University town with 13th century Castle and 12th century Cathedral, St Andrews Museum, St Andrews Aquarium, Craigtoun Country Park, East Sands Leisure Centre • Bowling, tennis, putting, and (of course) GOLF (British Golf Museum) • Theatre, cinema, arts centre. • Fun town tours, sandcastle building competitions (summer months).

i Tourist Information Centre,
70 Market Street, St Andrews KY16 9NU
01334 472021
e-mail: Standrews@visitscotland.com
www.visitfife.com

Beaches

• **WEST SANDS.** Wide, flat sandy beach. Within walking distance of town centre, ample parking. *Safety and maintenance:* cleaned regularly and patrolled by council staff; lifeguards during summer months. *Beach facilities:* catering outlets; toilets. *Dog restrictions:* banned from most of beach in summer months; dog exercise area.

• **EAST SANDS.** Sandy beach, just past the harbour; parking. *Safety and maintenance:* cleaned regularly; lifeguards during summer months. *Beach facilities:* catering facilities; watersports; toilets. *Dog restrictions:* banned during summer months.

Balmedie Beach, Aberdeenshire

★ Fun for all the Family ★

NORTHERN SCOTLAND

◆ **Anderson's Storybook Glen, Maryculter, near Aberdeen (01224 732941).** Old Woman's Shoe, Pixie Park, Old MacDonald, play park and the Three Bears' House.
www.storybookglenaberdeen.co.uk

◆ **Archaeolink Prehistory Park, near Insch (01464 851500).** All-weather attraction with events inside and out, exhibition and film theatre, all set in 40 acres.
www.archaeolink.co.uk

◆ **Cawdor Castle, Nairn (01667 404401).** A 14th century Keep, fortified in the 15th century and the 17th century, the massive fortress is set in splendid grounds with nature trails and gardens. Shops, snack bar, picnic area, restaurant and golf course.
www.cawdorcastle.com

◆ **Eilean Donan Castle, near Kyle of Lochalsh (01599 555202).** Probably the most photographed castle in Scotland, Eilean Donan stands in a romantic and picturesque setting on Loch Duich.
www.eieandonancastle.com

◆ **Glamis Castle, near Forfar (01307 840393).** Childhood home of the Queen Mother and birthplace of Princess Margaret. Visitors have a choice of admission to the Castle/grounds/formal garden/coach house/nature trail/picnic areas, including a children's play area.
www.glamis-castle.co.uk

◆ **Highland Wildlife Park, Kincraig (01540 651270).** Over 250 acres with red deer, European bison, wild horses, roe deer, Soay sheep, Highland cattle, wandering freely amidst magnificent Highland scenery.
www.highlandwildlifepark.org

◆ **Landmark Visitor Centre, Carrbridge (0800 731 3446).** Attractions include tree-top trail, pine forest nature centre, woodland maze and adventure playground with giant slide and aerial walkways.
www.landmark-centre.co.uk

◆ **The Loch Ness Exhibition Centre, Drumnadrochit (01456 450573).** Explore the mysteries surrounding the existence (or not!) of Nessie, the world-famous monster.
www.lochness.com

◆ **Timespan Heritage Centre, Helmsdale (01431 821327).** Award-winning heritage centre telling the dramatic story of the Highlands. Landscaped garden with collection of rare herbal medicinal plants.
www.timespan.org.uk

Other specialised holiday guides from **FHG**

PUBS & INNS OF BRITAIN
COUNTRY HOTELS OF BRITAIN
WEEKEND & SHORT BREAKS
IN BRITAIN & IRELAND
THE GOLF GUIDE
WHERE TO PLAY, WHERE TO STAY
500 GREAT PLACES TO STAY IN BRITAIN
SELF-CATERING HOLIDAYS
BED & BREAKFAST STOPS IN BRITAIN
PETS WELCOME!
CARAVAN & CAMPING HOLIDAYS
IN BRITAIN

Published annually: available in all good bookshops or direct from the publisher:

e-mail: admin@fhguides.co.uk
www.holidayguides.com

Scotland

☆ Fun for all the Family ☆

CENTRAL SCOTLAND

◆ **Bannockburn Heritage Centre, near Stirling (01786 812664).** Superb audio visual presentation and magnificent equestrian statue of Robert the Bruce.
www.nts.org.uk/bannockburn

◆ **Blair Drummond Safari & Adventure Park (01786 841456).** Drive through animal reserves, monkey jungle. Pets farm – even a boat safari round chimp island – plus rides, amusements .
www.blairdrummond.comk

◆ **British Golf Museum, St Andrews (01334 460046).** Relive all the history and atmosphere of 500 years of golf. Themed galleries feature the tournaments, players and equipment which today's game.
www.britishgolfmuseum.co.uk

◆ **Deep Sea World, North Queensferry (01383 411880).** An underwater safari beneath the Firth of Forth gives a superb view of thousands of fish as they travel along the longest underwater tunnel in the world.
www.deepseaworld.com

◆ ✳✳✳ **Falkirk Wheel (08700 500208).** A mechanical marvel, the world's only rotating boatlift used to connect the Forth & Clyde and Union canals.
www.thefalkirkwheel.co.uk

◆ **Frigate Unicorn, Victoria Dock, Dundee (01382 200900).** An 1824 wooden, 46 gun frigate; Britain's oldest ship afloat restored as a floating museum.
www.frigateunicorn.org

◆ **Museum of Transport, Kelvin Hall, Glasgow (0141-287 2720).** The oldest cycle in the world, trams, bikes, trains, horse drawn vehicles, special displays, models and more.
www.glasgowmuseums.com

◆ **New Lanark, Near Lanark (01555 661345).** An insight into the lives of working men and women in this restored conservation village in an attractive situation by the Falls of Clyde. A World Heritage site.
www.newlanark.org

◆ **Our Dynamic Earth, Edinburgh (0131 550 7800).** Charting the Earth's development over the last 4,500 million years with lots of interactive entertainment for adults and children.
www.dynamicearth.co. uk

◆ **St Andrews Aquarium (01334 474786).** Hundreds of different species in displays intended to re-create their natural habitat. Includes playful seals and colourful tropical fish.
www.standrewsaquarium.co.uk

◆ **Scottish Fisheries Museum, Anstruther (01333 310628).** A unique record of Scotland's fishing industry. Museum shop and tearoom. Restored fisherman's cottage.
www.scottishfishmuseum.org

◆ **Scottish Deer Centre, near Cupar (01337 810391).** Outdoor and indoor play areas and the chance to study (and stroke) these beautiful animals at close quarters. Also spectacular Wolf Wood.

☆ Fun for all the Family ☆

SOUTHERN SCOTLAND

◆ **Brodick Castle, Garden and Country Park (0844 493 2152).** Former seat of the Dukes of Hamilton (now NTS) with fine examples of silver, porcelain and paintings. Woodland walks, formal garden; ranger service.
www.nts.org.uk

◆ **Burns National Heritage Park, Alloway (01292 443700).** Burns Cottage Museum, Auld Kirk, Tam O' Shanter Experience, Brig O' Doon, Burns Monument and Gardens — all within half a mile of each other.
www.burnsheritagepark.com

◆ **Culzean Castle and Country Park, By Maybole (08701 181945).** 6000 years in one day. Castle designed by Robert Adam in 1777; park with deer, swans, walled garden, aviary, restaurant and tearoom.
www.culzeanexperience.org

◆ **Floors Castle, Kelso (01573 223333).** Scotland's largest inhabited castle with magnificent collections of tapestries, furniture and porcelain. Gift shop and restaurant.
www.roxburghe.net

◆ **Harestanes Countryside Visitor Centre, Jedburgh (01835 830306).** Wildlife garden and temporary exhibitions. Games and puzzles, adventure play area, tearoom, gift shop. Woodland walks.
www.scotborders.gov.ukt

◆ **Kelburn Castle & Country Centre, Fairlie (01475 568685).** Historic home of the Earls of Glasgow, with beautiful garden walks, tea room, pony trekking, adventure course, children's stockade, pets' corner and The Secret Forest.
www.kelburnestate.com

◆ **Loudoun Castle Theme Park, Galston (01563 822296).** Fun for all the family, with amusements and rides (including Britain's largest carousel), castle ruin, animals, aviary, restaurant and gift shop.
www.loudouncastle-online.co.uk

◆ **Magnum Leisure Centre, Irvine (01294 278381).** Leisure pool, ice rink, sports hall, fitness suite, fast food outlet, theatre/cinema and soft play area.
www.naleisure.co.uk

◆ **Traquair House, Near Innerleithen (01896 830323).** Oldest inhabited historic mansion in Scotland. Treasures date from 12th century, unique secret staircase to Priest's Room, craft workshop, woodland walks, maze, brewery.
www.traquair.co.uk

◆ **Thirlestane Castle, Lauder (01578 722430).** Border country life exhibitions in magnificent castle. Historic toys, woodland walk and picnic areas. Tearoom and gift shop.
www.thirlestanecastle.co.uk

◆ **Vikingar! Largs (01475 689777).** Let live Viking guides take you on an enthralling multi-media journey back in time to trace the history of the Vikings in Scotland. Also swimming pool, soft play area, cinema/theatre and cafe/bar.
www.naleisure.co.uk

the Pines
Country Guest House

Lynn and Dave welcome you to their home, and offer you personal service in a warm, cosy, friendly atmosphere. We provide the best of Highland hospitality.

all home cooking using local fresh produce • traditional or vegetarian meals special diets by arrangement • picnic lunches on request.

The house is centrally heated throughout. Family, double, twin en suite rooms, all with tea/coffee facilities, colour TV, radio alarm. No smoking. Open all year.

Children and pets welcome • Babysitting service available.
B&B from £30 daily • DB&B from £268 weekly.

**The Pines Country Guest House
Duthil, Carrbridge, Inverness-shire PH23 3ND
e-mail: lynn@thepines-duthil.co.uk
Tel / Fax: 01479 841220 • www.thepines-duthil.co.uk**

This quiet Victorian former rectory provides the ideal location for touring. Ideal base for golf enthusiasts, within easy reach of 46 golf courses and only 14 miles from St Andrews. 40 minutes from Edinburgh Airport, Perth and 30-35 minutes from Dundee.

Facilities include three en suite rooms – one double, one twin, one family (sleeps three to four), one family (sleeps three) with private bathroom. Colour TV and tea/coffee facilities in all rooms, cot available. Visitors' lounge with TV • Most credit cards accepted • Open all year. Terms from £30pppn • Non-smoking.

**Mrs Pam MacDonald, Dunclutha Guest House,
16 Victoria Road, Leven KY8 4EX
Tel: 01333 425515 • Fax: 01333 422311
e-mail: pam.leven@blueyonder.co.uk • www.dunclutha.myby.co.uk**

Scotland

Mount View Caravan Park

Luxury holiday homes for hire on caravan park set in peaceful, unspoilt countryside with beautiful views of the Clyde valley. Good for walking, cycling, fishing, golf and touring the area. Near to Moffat, Biggar, Edinburgh, Glasgow and Scottish Borders.

Fully equipped holiday home including microwave, TV/DVD and with double glazing and central heating.

En suite shower room, lounge, dining area, kitchen, twin and double bedrooms. Bedding and towels can be provided at an extra cost.

Easy access, just five minutes from J13 of the M74 and a short walk from the village shop.

£170 to £350 per week.

Abington, South Lanarkshire ML12 6RW   Tel: 01864 502808
e-mail: info@mountviewcaravanpark.co.uk • www.mountviewcaravanpark.co.uk

Cairngorm Highland Bungalows

Glen Einich, 29 Grampian View,
Aviemore, Inverness-shire PH22 1TF
*Tel: 01479 810653 • Fax: 01479 810262
e-mail: linda.murray@virgin.net
www.cairngorm-bungalows.co.uk*

Beautifully furnished and well equipped bungalows ranging from one to four bedrooms. All have colour TV, video, DVD, microwave, cooker, washer-dryer, fridge and patio furniture. Some have log fires. Leisure facilities nearby include golf, fishing on the River Spey, swimming, sauna, jacuzzi, tennis, skating and skiing. Within walking distance of Aviemore. Ideal touring base. Children and pets welcome.

Phone for colour brochure.

Open all year.

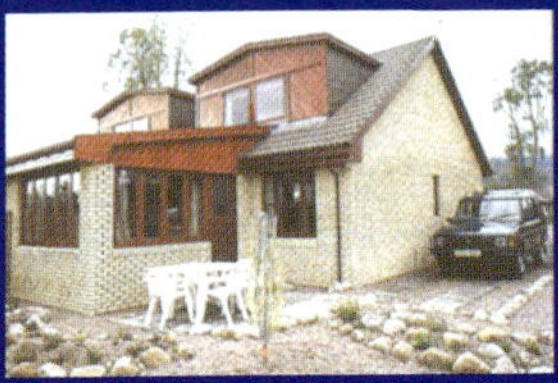

PITCAIRLIE HOUSE — Hidden Secret of Fife

Luxury Self Catering Holiday Cottage and Apartments near St Andrews in the Kingdom of Fife

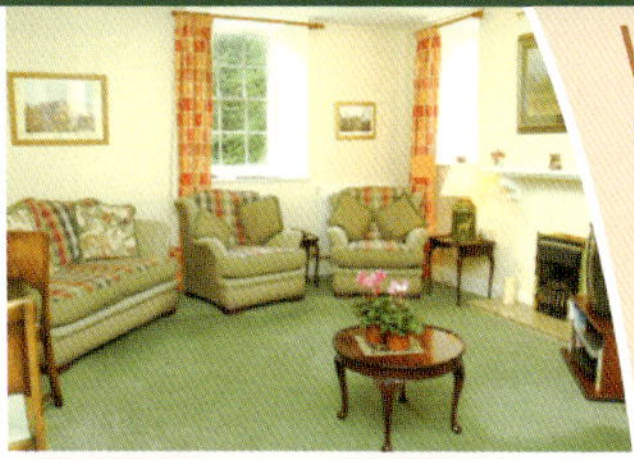

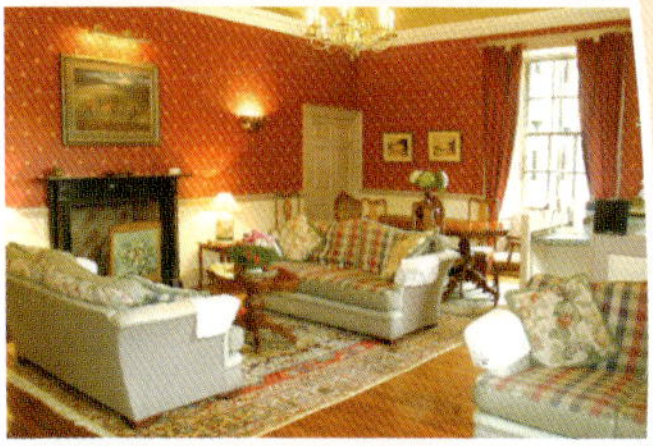

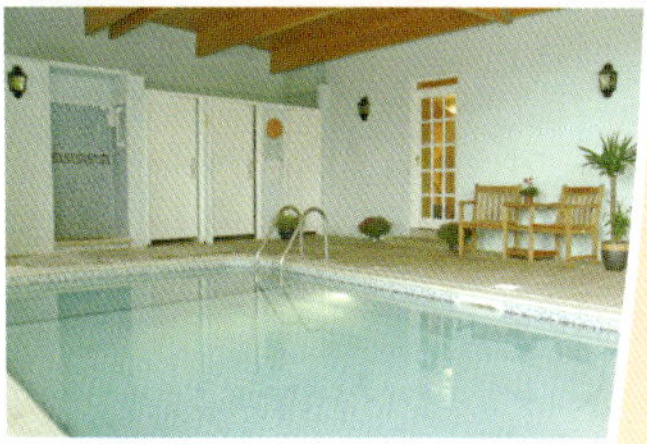

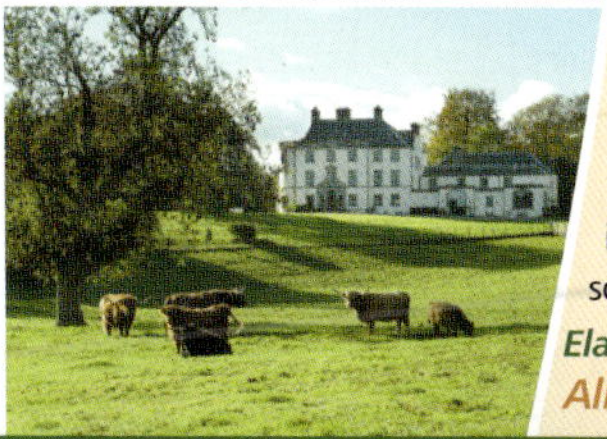

Welcome to the Kingdom of Fife

Set within a 120 acre estate of woods, streams, parklands and two ornamental lakes, Pitcairlie is a 16th century castle offering luxury self catering holiday cottage accommodation near St Andrews in Fife.

There are four self catering holiday apartments within the mansion and the original lodge house provides one further holiday cottage.

All of our properties have been newly refurbished to a very high standard, including fully fitted kitchens and gas central heating. Each has been awarded a 4 Star rating by VisitScotland. Our guests are welcome to enjoy our indoor heated swimming pool and sauna. Free Wi-Fi. All linen and heating provided.

Besides our holiday apartments and holiday cottage, we now offer Pitcairlie as a very special, historic venue for weddings, corporate events and hospitality, and groups.

Perhaps the best facility of all is the peace and quiet of Pitcairlie. Guests can enjoy walking in our secluded 120 acre estate with its woods, streams and lakes. The parklands are grazed by rare-bred sheep and Highland cattle. There is also a children's play area.

This lovely rural location is on the Perthshire / Fife border, two miles from Auchtermuchty. Just six miles away is the historic, medieval village of Falkland, home to Falkland Palace, a royal hunting lodge with connections to Mary Queen of Scots. An ideal area for rambling, hillwalking and exploring the East Neuk of Fife, with its sandy beaches and picturesque fishing villages all at hand. For golfers, there are many excellent golf courses within easy reach, including the Old Course in St Andrews and Carnoustie in Tayside.

St Andrews is an ancient university town, famous the world over as the home of golf. From Pitcairlie, the M9 is near at hand, allowing easy access to Edinburgh and the south, as well as north to Perth and the Scottish Highlands.

Eland Apartment awarded Gold Award for Excellence
All major credit/debit cards accepted

Pitcairlie House, Auchtermuchty, Fife KY14 6EU
Tel: 01337 827418 • Mobile: 07831 646157
e-mail: reservations@pitcairlie-leisure.co.uk • www.pitcairlie-leisure.co.uk

SPEYSIDE LEISURE PARK
Self-Catering Holidays in the Heart of the Highlands

The park is situated in a quiet riverside setting with mountain views, only a short walk from Aviemore centre and shops. We offer a range of warm, well equipped chalets, cabins and caravans, including a caravan for the disabled. Prices include electricity, gas, linen, towels and use of our heated indoor pool and sauna. There are swings, a climbing frame and low level balance beams for the children. Permit fishing is available on the river. Discounts are given on some local attractions.

Families, couples or groups will find this an ideal location for a wide range of activities including:

- **Horse riding • Golf • Fishing • Hillwalking**
- **RSPB Reserves • Mountain and Watersports • Reindeer herd**
- **Steam railway and the Whisky Trail**

Only slightly further afield you will find Culloden Moor, the Moray Firth dolphins and of course, the not to be missed, Loch Ness. Accommodation sleeps from 1-6, and we offer a reduced rate for a couple or one single person. Short Breaks are available.
Sorry, no pets, except guide and hearing dogs. No tents or camper vans.

Speyside Leisure Park
Dalfaber Road, Aviemore,
Inverness-shire PH22 1PX
Tel: 01479 810236
Fax: 01479 811688
e-mail:
fhg@speysideleisure.com
www.speysideleisure.com

Scotland 141

Rosehaugh Estate

Set in the beautiful countryside of Rosehaugh Estate on Ross-shire's Black Isle near the historic fishing village of Avoch, and around 15 miles from Inverness, we are pleased to offer a range of unique, high quality holiday homes. All our properties sleep 4 or 6 people, are spacious, luxuriously furnished and lavishly equipped. The properties are very different from each other, since each one is an historic Estate building which has played its own important role in past times.

The Boat House • Otter Lodge
Red Kite House • Bay Farm Cottages

For details contact Julie Metcalfe, Country Cottage Holiday,
137 Scalby Road, Scarborough YO12 6TB • Tel: 01723 373461
info@countrycottageholiday.com • www.rosehaugh-holidays.co.uk

The Trossachs

Loch View Barn, Craigard & Auld Toll Cottages

Four attractive units in the beautiful Trossachs, the most scenic part of Scotland's first National Park.

Auld Toll Cottages (Sleep 3 & 4). Rural situation west of Callander near a country pub and two woollen mills with tea rooms. The Callander/Strathyre cycle track is nearby providing attractive riverside walks and cycleways. Cycle storage available.

Craigard Apartment (Sleeps 2). Modern ground floor flat - own entrance door. Quiet central location. Private parking. Short easy walk to the Main Street with its varied shops, restaurants and other places of interest.

Lochview Barn (Sleeps 3). Well equipped barn conversion overlooking Loch Lubnaig, seven miles from Callander.

STB ★★★/★★★★
Sorry, no smoking and no pets.
Self-catering available:
low season £175 to £300 per week.
high season £250 to £450 per week

For more information or to make a reservation contact:
Drew or Kathleen Little
Riverview, Leny Road,
Callander FK17 8AL
Tel: 01877 330635

e-mail: drew@visitcallander.co.uk • www.visitcallander.co.uk

Scotland

BAREND HOLIDAY VILLAGE — SANDYHILLS, DALBEATTIE DG5 4NU

Escape to the beautiful South West Colvend coast, the perfect base for walking, touring and cycling in Dumfries & Galloway, which is Scotland in miniature, and only one hour's drive from England.

Our chalets, situated only a short walk from Sandyhills beach, are well equipped and centrally heated for all year comfort. Pets welcome or pet-free. Their decks overlook our loch or Colvend 18-hole golf course, and the surrounding countryside teems with wildlife - red squirrels, badgers and deer are our neighbours.

On-site boules courts, bar, restaurant, sauna and indoor pool. Wifi internet access available.

3 days minimum: any day of entry, prices include linen and swimming. From £264 for four for 3 days.

Tel: 01387 780663
www.barendholidayvillage.co.uk

High standard accommodation in Dunkeld, Perthshire, sleeping 2-8

Golden Pond offers an opportunity to stay in a newly built Scandinavian log cabin, nestling in 3 acres of stunning countryside in the Atholl Estates. Close to the Loch of the Lowes Nature Reserve and surrounded by breathtaking scenery of lochs and glens, it is the perfect location for birdwatchers, hillwalkers and fishermen, or just to get away from it all in a peaceful tranquil setting. Excellent base for families, couples or groups. Within easy daily reach of Aviemore, Inverness, Aberdeen or Edinburgh.

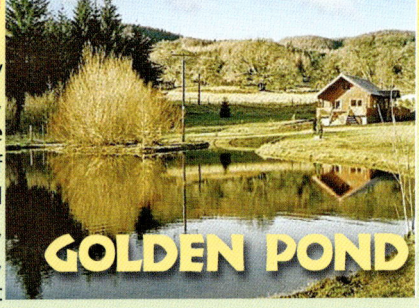

Enquiries, please tel: 01350 727137 • e-mail: katehowie1@yahoo.co.uk • www.hattongrange.com

The Queen's View across Loch Tummel, Perthshire

Scotland

19th century Minard Castle beside Loch Fyne is a peaceful location for a quiet break. Stroll in the grounds, walk by the loch, explore the woods, or tour this scenic area with lochs, hills, gardens, castles and historic sites.
THE LODGE • a comfortable bungalow with small garden and view through trees to the loch, sleeps 4-6.
THE MEWS APARTMENT • sleeps 4-5.
• Well equipped; central heating, hot water, linen and towels included.
• Terms £140 to £390 per week. Open all year.

Also Four Star B&B in Minard Castle; from £60pppn, open April-Oct.

Minard Castle
SELF-CATERING
Minard, Inveraray PA32 8YB
Tel & Fax: 01546 886272
reinoldgayre@minardcastle.com
www.minardcastle.com

Dunroamin
Caravan Park
Main Street, Lairg IV27 4AR

Lew Hudson, his wife Margaret and their family welcome you to Dunroamin Caravan Park.

A small family-run park situated in the picturesque village of Lairg by Loch Shin, this is the ideal base for touring the whole of Sutherland and Caithness. Fishing and walking nearby, with golf just 15 miles away.

Outstandingly well maintained grounds with Crofters licensed restaurant on site.

Electric hook-ups. 200 yards from pub, bank, shops, post office, etc.
Holiday caravans for hire, tourers and tents welcome.

Tel: 01549 402447

enquiries@lairgcaravanpark.co.uk
www.lairgcaravanpark.co.uk

Scotland

Hillhead Caravans Achmelvich

Excellent self-catering accommodation at the beautiful white, safe, sandy beach of Achmelvich, near Lochinver in North West Scotland, one of the country's beauty spots. Ideal for family holidays.

Clean, modern, 6-berth, fully serviced caravans to let, 150 metres from the beach.

Our accommodation and area are perfect for country lovers and a good centre for hillwalking, photography, cycling, climbing, caving, geology, swimming, bird-watching, touring, fishing, sailing – or just relaxing with a good book! Open late March to late October.

Details from Durrant and Maysie Macleod

Hillhead Caravans • Lochinver IV27 4JA

Tel: 01571 844206 • Fax: 01571 844454
e-mail: info@lochinverholidays.co.uk
www.lochinverholidays.co.uk

Inchmurrin is the largest island on Loch Lomond and offers a unique experience. Three self-catering apartments, sleeping from four to six persons, and a detached cedar clad cottage sleeping eight, are available. The well appointed apartments overlook the garden, jetties and the loch beyond. Inchmurrin is the ideal base for watersports and is situated on a working farm.

Terms from £407 to £850 per week, £281 to £560 per half week.

A ferry service is provided for guests, and jetties are available for customers with their own boats. Come and stay and have the freedom to roam and explore anywhere on the island.

Inchmurrin Island SELF-CATERING HOLIDAYS

e-mail: scotts@inchmurrin-lochlomond.com
www.inchmurrin-lochlomond.com
Inchmurrin Island, Loch Lomond G63 0JY
Tel: 01389 850245 • Fax: 01389 850513

Irresistible Orkney

Hostel, Caravan and Camping Accommodation

Warbeth Beach overlooking the Hoy Hills

Point of Ness Caravan & Camping Site, Stromness
Stromness is a small picturesque town with impressive views of the hills of Hoy. The site is one mile from the harbour in a quiet, shoreline location. Many leisure activities are available close by, including fishing, sea angling, golf and a swimming & fitness centre.

Contact: stromnesscashoffice@orkney.gov.uk or recreation@orkney.gov.uk
www.orkney.gov.uk • Tel: 01856 850262

Birsay Outdoor Centre / Caravan & Camping Site
A new campsite located on the 3-Star hostel site in the picturesque north west of Orkney.

Hoy Centre
Four Star hostel accommodation with en suite facilities.
Ideal base for exploring Hoy's magnificent scenery and natural environment.

Rackwick Hostel
Rackwick is considered one of the most beautiful places in Orkney with towering cliffs and steep heathery hills. This cosy hostel has spectacular views over Rackwick's cliffs and beach.

For Birsay, Hoy and Rackwick contact recreation@orkney.gov.uk
Tel: 01856 873535 • www.hostelsorkney.co.uk

The Pickaquoy Centre and Camping Park, Kirkwall
Tel: 01856 879900

A 4-Star touring park with the latest in park amenities is situated at the Pickaquoy Centre complex, an impressive leisure facility offering a range of activities for all the family. Within walking distance of the St Magnus Cathedral and Kirkwall town centre.

e-mail: enquiries@pickaquoy.com • www.pickaquoy.co.uk

Scotland

An Sabhal Cottages
Portnahaven, Isle of Islay

The cottages have been recently developed to offer every modern comfort. They are situated midway between the twin picturesque fishing villages of Portnahaven and Port Wemyss.
Both cottages (each sleeps 6) are contained within the one building with separate access. The bedrooms are on the ground floor; large lounge on the upper floor. Fully fitted kitchens, bathrooms, WC and shower rooms. The upstairs lounges are comfortably furnished and have TV, DVD and videos. Central heating throughout. Exceptional views across to the Rhinns lighthouse and the Donegal coast.

For bookings, please contact Mrs Mona MacArthur
Tel: 01496 860293 • mona@ansabhalcottages.co.uk
www.ansabhalcottages.co.uk

PORTPATRICK HOLIDAYS

We currently have six 4-Star holiday units ranging from one to five bedrooms. All houses are fully equipped to a very high standard and enjoy magnificent views over the sea to Ireland and Dunskey Glen. **Tel: 01776 810555**
info@portpatrickholidays.co.uk
www.portpatrickholidays.co.uk
47 Main Street, Portpatrick DG9 8JW

The Falkirk Wheel, Stirlingshire

WALES

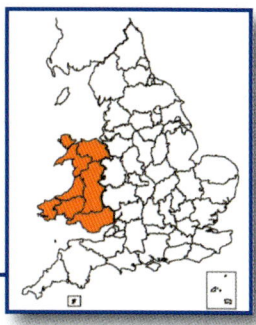

🏰 Best Beaches 🏰

An outstanding number resort beaches in Wales have been awarded the European Blue Flag for 2009, and an equally impressive number have received Seaside Awards (Resort and Rural Categories). Seaside Awards are given to well-managed beaches which comply with the legal minimum microbiological standards of water quality.

BLUE FLAG BEACHES 2009

- **ANGLESEY**
  Benllech, Church Bay, Llanddona, Porth, Llanddwyn, Newborough, Dafarch
- **GWYNEDD**
  Abersoch, Abermaw, Barmouth, Tywyn, Pwllheli, Fairbourne, Dinas Dinlle
- **NORTH WALES**
  Prestatyn, Rhos-on-Sea/Colwyn Bay
- **CARMARTHENSHIRE**
  Pendine
- **CEREDIGION**
  Aberystwyth (North), Aberystwyth (South), New Quay (Harbour),
- **PEMBROKESHIRE**
  Broadhaven (North), Dale, Lydstep, Saundersfoot, Newgale, Newport, Tenby (North), Tenby (South), St Davids (Whitesands), Poppit Sands
- **South Wales**
  Bracelet Bay, Caswell Bay, Langland Bay, Porthcawl (Rest Bay), Port Eynon

ℹ️ **VisitWales**
- **Tel: 08708 300306**
- **Fax: 08701 211259**
- **e-mail: info@visitwales.com**
- **www.visitwales.co.uk**

Colwyn Bay beach, North Wales

Wales

ABERYSTWYTH

Family Fun Activities: Sports and leisure centre, swimming pools, children's playgrounds, parks, promenade, outdoor paddling pool • Narrow gauge railway, electric cliff railway, camera obscura, marina, castle, hill fort, National Library of Wales, museum, theatre, cinema • Nature reserves and forestry centres, farm park, boat trips, coastal paths, cycle path.

i Tourist Information Centre, Terrace Road, Aberystwyth SY23 2AG
01970 612125 • Fax: 01970 626566
aberystwythtic@ceredigion.gov.uk
www.tourism.ceredigion.gov.uk

Beaches

• **BEACH.** Two-award-winning sloping beaches of coarse grey sand and shingle; North Beach fronted by promenade, parking on sea front; South Beach has ample parking. *Safety and maintenance:* water quality on both beaches usually good. Beach Officer/lifeguard usually on duty July/August. *Beach facilities:* rock pools, donkey rides; paddling pool etc on promenade; restaurants and kiosks; toilets. *Dog restrictions:* dogs banned between 1st May and 30th September on North Beach between jetty and Constitution Hill, and on South Beach between Castle headland and first groyne on South Marine Terrace

COLWYN BAY & RHOS-ON-SEA

Family Fun Activities: Welsh Mountain Zoo, Eirias Park with leisure centre, swimming pool, picnic and play areas, boating lake, model yacht pond, indoor tennis centre and skateboarding area • Pier and promenade with cycle track, Puppet Theatre, cricket ground and children's outdoor paddling pool at Rhos-on-Sea • Angling, bowling, golf, walking, watersports • Theatre/cinema with shows all year round.

★ **Special Events:** May Bank Holiday: Bay of Colwyn Promenade Day. **August:** Festive Fridays - every Friday in August.

i Colwyn Bay Touch Screen, Imperial Buildings, Prince's Drive, Colwyn Bay.
Tourist Information Point, Happy Faces Centre, Promenade, Rhos-on-Sea
www.visitcolwynbay.org.uk

Beaches

• **BEACH.** Sandy beach with easy access along A55 expressway. *Beach facilities:* kiosks; & toilets operate using RADAR Key.

BRITAIN'S BEST BEACHES
See pages 8-11

FHG Guides

publish a large range of well-known accommodation guides.
We will be happy to send you details or you can use
the order form at the back of this book.

LLANDUDNO

Family Fun Activities: Pier • putting, paddling pool, indoor swimming pool, yacht pond • Alice in Wonderland memorial on West Shore promenade, tramway and cable car to Great Orme Country Park and Visitor Centre, Great Orme Copper Mines, boat trips, Punch & Judy, 10-pin bowling • Llandudno Museum, Alice in Wonderland Visitor Centre, Bodafon Farm Park, Ski & Snowboard Centre with toboggan run • Theatre, art gallery • Victorian shopping centre.

Special Events: **May Bank Holiday:** Victorian Extravaganza. **June:** Gwyl Llandudno Festival - a summer arts festival. **July:** vehicle rally; Fun day, Bodafon Fields; various promenade events. **November:** Celtic Winter Fayre.

Tourist Information Centre, Chapel Street, Llandudno LL30 2UY
01492 876413
e-mail: llandudnotic@conwy.gov.uk
www.llandudno-tourism.co.uk

Beaches

• **NORTH SHORE BEACH.** Two miles long, sand and shingle, naturally sheltered; promenade and pier with amusements etc. *Safety and maintenance:* safe bathing beach. *Beach facilities:* deck chairs, donkey rides; pub and hotels on promenade; ice cream kiosks, snack bars etc nearby; toilets with & access at eastern end.

• **WEST SHORE BEACH.** Sandy beach, one mile long; promenade and parking. *Safety and maintenance:* warning signs (sand banks can be dangerous on incoming tide). *Beach facilities:* children's play area; snack bar.

PORTHCAWL

Family Fun Activities: A variety of activities ranging from sports to all the fun of the fair.

Special Events: **February:** Celtic Festival of Wales. **April:** Porthcawl Jazz Festival. **July/August:** Porthcawl Town Carnival; Sea Festival. **September:** Elvis Festival.

Heritage Coast Tourist Information Centre, Old Police Station, John Street, Porthcawl CF36 3DT • 01656 786639
e-mail: porthcawltic@bridgend.gov.uk
www.visitbridgend.com

Beaches

• **BEACHES.** Trecco Bay and Rest Bay offer miles of golden sands; parking and good disabled access. *Beach facilities:* deckchairs; cafes and ice-cream kiosks; toilets nearby in town. *Dog restrictions:* banned in summer from June onwards.

TENBY

Family Fun Activities: Safe, sandy beaches • Leisure centre, amusement arcade, bowls, putting, sailing, pony trekking, golf courses • Pavilion (plays, variety shows, dancing, concerts etc), male voice choir concerts • Museum and art gallery, 15th century Tudor Merchant's House, aquarium, art galleries • The town is pedestrianised during July and August.

Special Events: Air Sea Rescue and Helicopter Displays; Winter and Summer Carnivals, brass bands, Arts Festival.

Information Centre, Tenby
01834 842402
tenby.tic@pembrokeshire.gov.uk

☆ Fun for all the Family ☆

◆ **Anglesey Sea Zoo, Brynsiencyn (01248 430411).** Meet the fascinating creatures that inhabit the seas and shores around Anglesey; adventure playground, children's activities, shops and restaurants.
www.angleseyseazoo.co.uk

◆ **Bodafon Farm Park, Llandudno (01492 549060).** Enjoy a tractor/trailer ride around the paddocks and see the variety of rare breed animals, including shire horses, llamas, and peacocks. Shop, cafe and adventure playground.
www.bodafon.co.uk

◆ **Henblas Park, Bodorgan (01407 840440).** Situated in the heart of Anglesey, with lots to see and do - shearing demonstrations, duck display, indoor adventure playground, farm animals - entertainment for the whole family, whatever the weather.
www.nwt.co.uk

◆ **Pili Palas Nature World, Anglesey (01248 712474).** Exotic butterflies and birds in natural settings, plus (the children's favourites!) creepy crawlies and reptiles. Picnic area, cafe and adventure playground.
www.pilipalas.co.uk

◆ **Rhyl Seaquarium (01745 344660).** Spectacular underwater tunnel allows you to walk through sharks, stingrays and other sea creatures. New Sealion Cove.
www.rhyl.com/sealife

◆ **Snowdon Mountain Railway, Llanberis (0871 720 0033).** Travel by train on Britain's only rack and pinion railway up Snowdon, the highest mountain in England and Wales. New Summit Visitor Centre.
www.snowdonrailway.co.uk

◆ **Sygun Copper Mine, Beddgelert (01766 890595).** Stalagmites and stalactites formed from ferrous oxide. Award-winning attraction with underground audio visual tours.
www.syguncoppermine.co.uk

◆ **Welsh Mountain Zoo, Colwyn Bay (01492 532938).** Magnificent animals in natural surroundings, plus Chimpanzee World, Jungle Adventureland and Tarzan Trail, children's farm, etc - a great day out.
www.welshmountainzoo.org

Other specialised holiday guides from FHG

PUBS & INNS OF BRITAIN • **COUNTRY HOTELS** OF BRITAIN
WEEKEND & SHORT BREAKS IN BRITAIN & IRELAND
THE GOLF GUIDE WHERE TO PLAY, WHERE TO STAY
500 GREAT PLACES TO STAY IN BRITAIN
SELF-CATERING HOLIDAYS IN BRITAIN
BED & BREAKFAST STOPS IN BRITAIN • **PETS WELCOME!**
CARAVAN & CAMPING HOLIDAYS IN BRITAIN

Published annually: available in all good bookshops or direct from the publisher:
e-mail: admin@fhguides.co.uk • www.holidayguides.com

☆ Fun for all the Family ☆

◆ **Borth Animalarium, Borth (01970 871224).** Domestic and farm animals in the petting barn; exoic and endangered species in large enclosures. Pony rides and handling sessions. Indoor and outdoor play areas; cafe and shop
www.animalarium.co.uk

◆ **Centre for Alternative Technology, Machynlleth (01654 705950).** A "green" village with displays of sustainable and renewable sources of power eg solar, wind. Energy saving houses, organic gardens, bookshop. Adventure playground, restaurant.
www.cat.org.uk

◆ **Chwarel Hen Slate Caverns, Llanfair, Near Harlech (01766 780247).** Self-guided tours of awesome series of slate caverns – spooky in places, but memorable. Also children's farmyard.
www.llanfairslatecaverns.co.uk

◆ **Felinwynt Rainforest and Butterfly Centre, Rhosmaen, Near Aberporth (01239 810882).** Exotic butterflies flying freely in a hothouse atmosphere amid tropical plants and the taped sounds of a Peruvian rainforest.
www.butterflycentre.co.uk

◆ **King Arthur's Labyrinth, Machynlleth (01654 761584).** Sail along an underground river into a world of mystery, legends and storytelling. Also Bards' Quest maze and Corris Craft Centre with many original crafts and workshops. Cafe, outdoor play area.
www.kingarthurslabyrinth.co.uk

◆ **Llywernog Silver-Lead Mine, Ponterwyd, Aberystwyth (01970 890620).** Underground tours and miners' trail telling the story of the hunt for gold and silver in the Welsh hills.
www.silverminetours.co.uk

◆ **Talyllyn Railway, Tywyn (01654 710472).** Historic steam-operated railway which runs through 7 miles of beautiful countryside, past the scenic Dolgoch Falls, to Abergynolwyn and Nant Gwernol. Railway shop, museum and tearoom.
www.talyllyn.co.uk

FHG Guides

Looking for holiday accommodation?
search for details of properties where children are welcome
www.holidayguides.com

Wales

★ Fun for all the Family ★

SOUTH WALES

◆ **Big Pit, Blaenavon (01495 790311).** Don a miner's helmet and go down a real coal mine with ex-miners as guides. See the stables where the pit ponies were kept. World Heritage Site.
www.museumwales.ac.uk

◆ **Cardiff Castle (029 2087 8100).** Spanning nearly 2000 years of history, the splendidly decorated apartments are set in a magnificent building surrounded by eight-acre grounds.
www.cardiffcastle.com

◆ **The Dinosaur Experience, Great Wedlock (01834 842668).** Unique Visitor Centre in 33 acre park, with life-size models, dinosaur trail, hands-on activities; restaurant; picnic areas.

◆ **Oakwood Theme Park, Narberth (01834 891373).** There's a whole voyage of discovery just waiting to set sail at Oakwood. With more than 40 rides and attractions set in 80 acres of landscaped gardens and parkland, there are absolutely no constraints on fun!
www.oakwoodthemepark.co.uk

◆ **Rhondda Heritage Park, Trehafod (01443 682036).** See the story of Black Gold unfold as you tour the site, set in former working colliery. Underground tour, display, visitor centre, tearoom and gift shop.
www.rhonddaheritagepark.com

◆ **Techniquest, Cardiff (029 2047 5475).** Where science and technology come to life - visitors are actively encouraged to handle the exhibits.
www.techniquest.org

Caldicot Castle & Country Park, Near Chepstow (01291 420241). Explore the castle's fascinating past with an audio tour, and take in the breathtaking views of the 55-acre grounds from the battlements. Children's activity centre, play area.
www.caldicotcastle.co.uk

Cantref Adventure Farm, Brecon (01874 665223). Award-winning family attraction with live shows, tractor and trailer rides, new paddle boats and electronic tractors, indoor play area, and Europe's longest sledge ride.
www.cantref.com

Cardiff Castle, South Wales

Wales

**Bron Celyn Guest House,
Lôn Muriau, Llanrwst Road,
Betws-y-Coed LL24 0HD
Tel: 01690 710333
Fax: 01690 710111**

A warm welcome awaits you at this delightful guest house overlooking the Gwydyr Forest and Llugwy/Conwy Valleys and village of Betws-y-Coed in Snowdonia National Park. Ideal centre for touring, walking, climbing, fishing and golf. Also excellent overnight stop en route for Holyhead ferries.
Easy walk into village and close to Conwy/Swallow Falls and Fairy Glen.

Most rooms en suite, all with colour TV and beverage makers • Lounge
Full central heating • Garden • Car park • Open all year • Full hearty breakfast, packed meals, evening meals - special diets catered for • Walkers and Cyclists Welcome.

***B&B from £24 to £35, reduced rates for children under 12 years.
Special out of season breaks.***

Jim and Lilian Boughton

e-mail: welcome@broncelyn.co.uk • www.broncelyn.co.uk

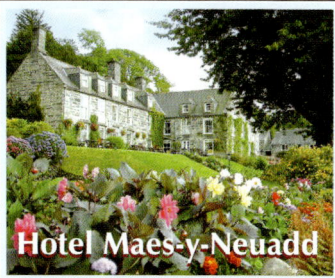

Hotel Maes-y-Neuadd

**Talsarnau, Near Harlech LL47 6YA
Tel: 01766 780200
Fax: 01766 780211
e-mail: maes@neuadd.com
www.neuadd.com**

A warm welcome awaits you at this historic Welsh manor house, nestled on a hillside in the heart of Snowdonia, with fabulous views of the mountains and coast. Dating back to 14th century, this beautiful granite building is now a 4-Star Gold Award country house hotel, set amongst 80 acres of gardens, parkland, forest and vegetable/kitchen gardens. Happily, 21st century amenities together with excellent friendly service ensure a relaxing and comfortable stay!

Ideally situated for exploring Snowdonia and its many attractions and with a range of rooms and prices to suit all tastes and budgets; an award-winning restaurant serving fresh local produce (much from our own gardens) and an excellent wine list – it's definitely a great place to stay and well worth paying us a visit!

We are open for morning coffee, lunch, afternoon tea, dinner or, if you fancy a treat, champagne and strawberries on the terrace!

Children welcome – children's menu, early teas, baby listening, family dining room.
Dogs also welcome in two of our Coach House rooms – dog sitting by arrangement.

**Good Hotel Guide
Country House Hotel
of the Year 2003**

Around the magnificent coast of Wales
Pembrokeshire, Cardigan Bay, Snowdonia, Anglesey, Lleyn Peninsula, Borders

Choose from over 300 Quality Cottages

Pets Welcome Free

A small specialist agency with over 40 years experience letting quality cottages.

Enjoy unashamed luxury in traditional Welsh Cottages. Situated near safe sandy beaches and in the heart of Wales — famed for scenery, walks, wild flowers, birds, badgers and foxes.

Pets welcome FREE at most of our properties

Leonard Rees, Quality Cottages, Cerbid, Solva, Haverfordwest, Pembrokeshire. SA62 6YE

**Telephone: (01348) 837871
for our FREE Colour Brochure**

www.qualitycottages.co.uk

100s of pictures of quality cottages and beautiful Wales

Wales

Little Slice of Heaven on the Coast - a perfect place for a family holiday or a relaxing short break.

Escape! Relax! Unwind! Explore! at Wales' Most Complete Resort

Exhilarating cliff-top walks, stunning scenery and the only Elemis Premier Spa in West Wales!

This magical location – once the 12th century estate of Lord St David – dominates the cliff-top overlooking Lydstep Bay and beautiful Caldey Island. Set in the only coastal National Park in the UK, the original whitewashed stone buildings have been recreated as luxury cottages.
Included in the price of your holiday are all our leisure facilities: a 9-hole golf course, indoor heated pool, hot-tub, gym, sauna, all-weather tennis courts and a children's adventure playground.
Children's activities on school holidays and several tourist attractions for children nearby.
Our Elemis Premier Spa has over 80 blissful treatments and holistic therapies guaranteed to relax your body and replenish your spirit. Our stylish Italian influenced restaurant Waves, with an amazing view of Caldey Island, serves à la carte dishes using locally sourced ingredients.

Lydstep, Near Tenby SA70 7SG • 01834 870000
www.celtichaven.co.uk • e-mail: welcome@celtichaven.com

Penffynnon Holiday Properties

This small cluster of self-contained properties enjoys a unique and special setting in the quiet holiday village of Aberporth on Cardigan Bay. All visitors are delighted when they first arrive and find out just how close they are to the water's edge - every one of our properties is within 200 yards of the sea. It's hard to imagine a more relaxing holiday.

DOLPHIN COTTAGE (pictured) is all on one level (Access Grade 2) and sleeps 6 in three bedrooms • **MORAWEL** has 5 bedrooms and 4 bathrooms, and sleeps 10 • **CILGWYN** has been converted into two self-contained villas, each with 3 bedrooms • **TY BROC** is a split level house to sleep 8.

All are very well equipped, and prices include bed linen, heating and lighting. Open all year.

Dolphin Cottage

For details contact: **Jann Tucker, Penffynnon, Aberporth, Ceredigion SA43 2DA**
Tel: 01239 810387 • Fax: 01239 811401 e-mail: jann@aberporth.com
www.aberporth.com

Wales

Islawrffordd
Caravan Park

Situated on the Snowdonia coastline, just north of Barmouth, our park offers a limited number of caravans for hire, most of which come with double glazing and central heating along with laundered bedding.

Our touring caravan field has been modernised to super pitch quality including hard standing with each plot being reservable.

Camping is also available on a first-come, first-served basis.

Park facilities include
- *shop • bar • laundry*
- *indoor heated pool*
- *new toilet block*
- *amusements • jacuzzi*
- *sauna • food bars*

Enquiries regarding any of the above to John or Jane.

Tel: 01341 247269
Fax: 01341 242639
e-mail: info@islawrffordd.co.uk
www.islawrffordd.co.uk

Tal-y-Bont, Gwynedd LL43 2BQ

Coastal Snowdonia
300 YARDS FROM LONG SANDY BEACH

ENJOY THE BEST OF BOTH WORLDS, BETWEEN SEA AND MOUNTAINS

LUXURY HOLIDAY HOMES FOR SALE AND HIRE

- Licensed Club House
- Pets Welcome
- Heated Swimming Pool
- Games Room
- Electrical Hook-ups available

- Super Pitches available
- Two Shower Blocks
- Two Children's Play Areas
- Touring & Camping on level grassland
- Washing-up and Laundry facilities

To request a brochure please contact:
Dinlle Caravan Park, Dinas Dinlle, Caernarfon LL54 5TS
Tel: 01286 830324
www.thornleyleisure.co.uk

ON THE COAST MID-WAY BETWEEN NEW QUAY & ABERAERON

Gilfach Holiday Village

Self Catering Holidays Overlooking the Sea

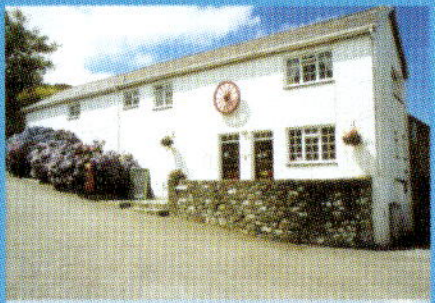
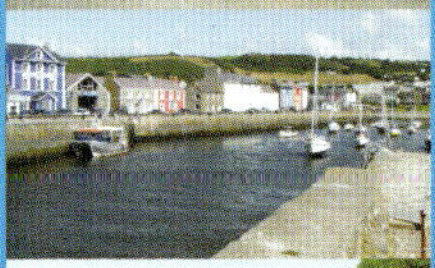
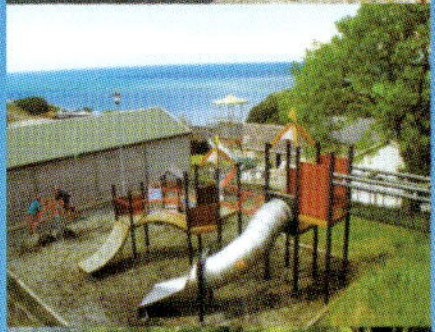
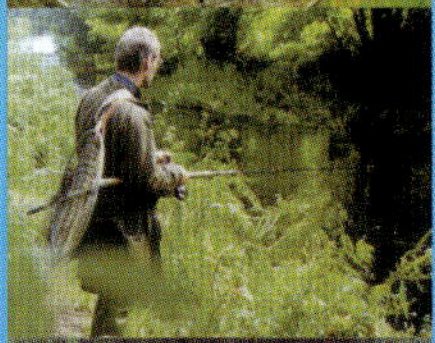
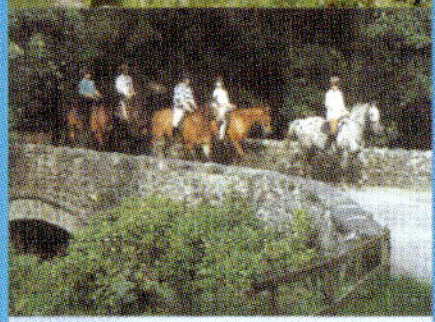
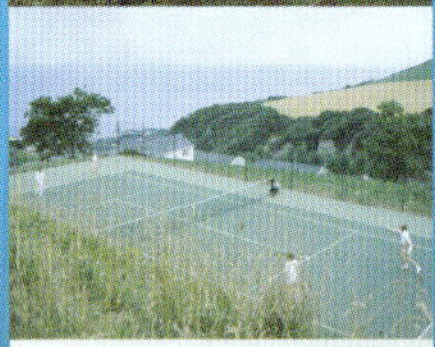
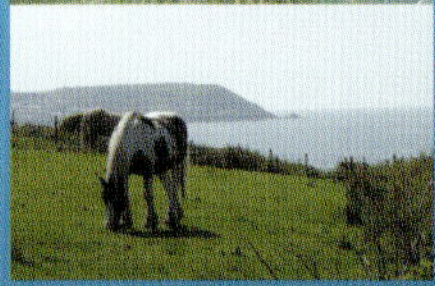

Escape to Glorious Gilfach

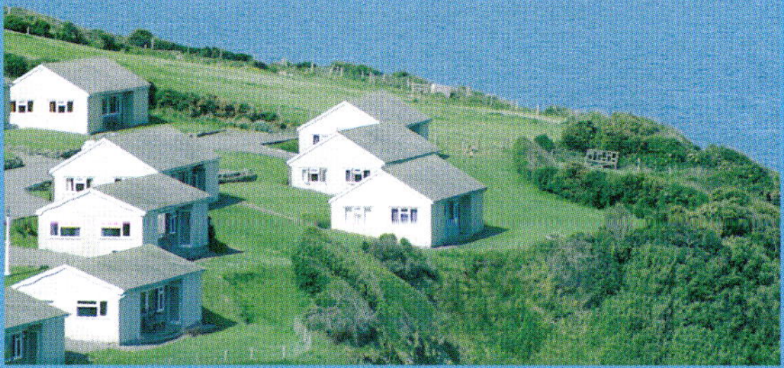

HORSE & PONY RIDING: PETS WELCOME

Nestling between the resorts of Aberaeron and New Quay in the superb countryside of West Wales, is a little gem of a holiday retreat. Directly overlooking the sea it is an idyllic haven for those who appreciate peace and seclusion. Yet if you feel in need of activity, there is much to offer.

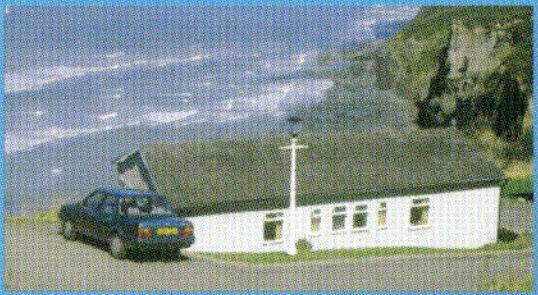
Bungalows overlooking the sea

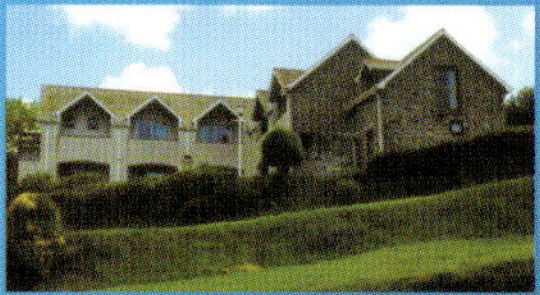
Superb views from the Apartments

Facilities include: Bungalows overlooking the sea
Own Private Beach • Private Bar • Kids Den
Children's Playground • Tennis Court • River/Sea Fishing
Horse & Pony Riding • Cliff walks and much, much more

There is a choice of modern Bungalows accommodating up to 6 persons and luxury 2/3 person Apartments, set in 36 acres of grounds.
Horse riding is available in The Village to suit all ages. Enjoy sea fishing trips or fish from the beach. River fishing is also available nearby. The Village has its own licensed club, en tout cas all-weather tennis court. The children have a den and playground and pets are welcome.

Direct website: www.selfcateringinwales.com
For our colour brochure please call: 01545 580 288

GILFACH HOLIDAY VILLAGE

Llwyncelyn, Nr. Aberaeron, Ceredigion SA46 0HN Tel: (01545) 580 288

www.stratfordcaravans.co.uk email: info@stratfordcaravans.co.uk

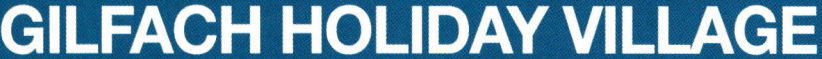

Wales

PEMBROKESHIRE NATIONAL PARK

Three-bedroom fully furnished holiday lodge, within easy walking distance of sandy beaches and the Coastal Footpath. Ideal centre for family holidays, walking, birdwatching. Sleeps 6 + cot.
From £140 to £375 per week.

MRS L.P. ASHTON, 10 ST LEONARDS ROAD, THAMES DITTON, SURREY KT7 0RJ
Tel: 020-8398 6349
e-mail: lejash@aol.com
www.33timberhill.com

Scamford Caravan Park • Peaceful family-run park

Close to the Coastal Path and lovely sandy beaches. 25 luxurious caravans with Four Star Tourist Board grading. Super playground. Pets welcome.

Richard & Christine White
Tel/Fax: 01437 710304 • www.scamford.com
e-mail: holidays@scamford.com

SCAMFORD CARAVAN PARK, KEESTON, HAVERFORDWEST SA62 6HN

Cae Berllan

Let Ann and Mike welcome you to their 17-acre smallholding situated three miles outside Caernarfon, with easy access to Snowdonia National Park. We offer three converted stone cottages, with all the requirements of modern day living.

On the farm we have horses and ponies, a few sheep and chickens. There is an orchard which is an ideal area for picnics and for children to play. There is also a play/sitting area at the back of the cottages which has secure gates. There is ample parking for cars, boats and jet skis. Stabling for horses is available, if you wish to follow the mountain and coastal bridle paths in the area. There is an extensive cycle path within one mile. Cottages sleep 4 to 7.

Carrag Bwa sleeps up to 7 in three bedrooms. Fully fitted kitchen/diner. Large lounge with French doors leading to enclosed garden.

Hendy & Ty Pen each sleep up to 4 in two bedrooms. Fully fitted kitchen/diner. Large lounge with French doors leading to patio area.

MRS A.M. OWENS, CAE BERLLAN, TYN LON, LLANDWROG, CAERNARFON LL54 5SN • 01286 830818
www.caeberllan.co.uk • mail@caeberllan.co.uk

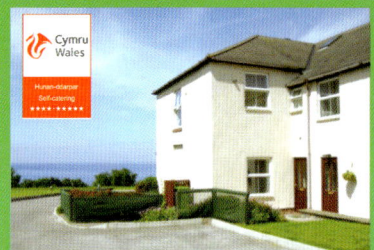

NORTH WALES HOLIDAYS

Cedarwood Chalets • Cottages • Coach House

High quality cottages, cosy chalets and large coach house for 2-9, overlooking sea at Bron-Y-Wendon or in picturesque valley at Nant-Y-Glyn. 16 units in total. Wide range of facilities with many leisure activities nearby. Short breaks all year. Pets welcome. Visit Wales 2-5 Stars.

Bron-Y-Wendon & Nant-Y-Glyn Holiday Parks,
Wern Road, Llanddulas, Colwyn Bay LL22 8HG
e-mail: stay@northwales-holidays.co.uk
www.northwales-holidays.co.uk

For colour brochures telephone:
01492 512903/ 512282
or visit our website

Cynllun Croeso Welcome Host GOLD

British Holiday & Home Parks Association

Cymru Wales Hunan-ddarpar Self-catering

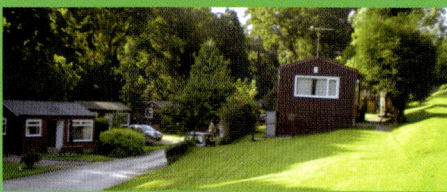

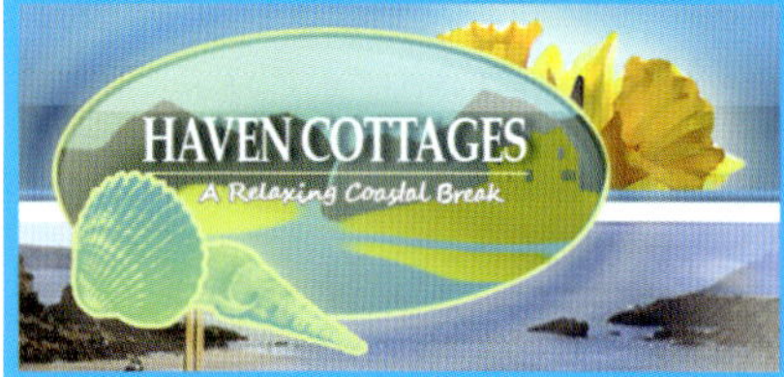

Haven Cottages

Sycamore Lodge

Nolton Haven SA62 3NH

Tel: 01437 710200

e-mail: info@havencottages.co.uk
www.havencottages.co.uk

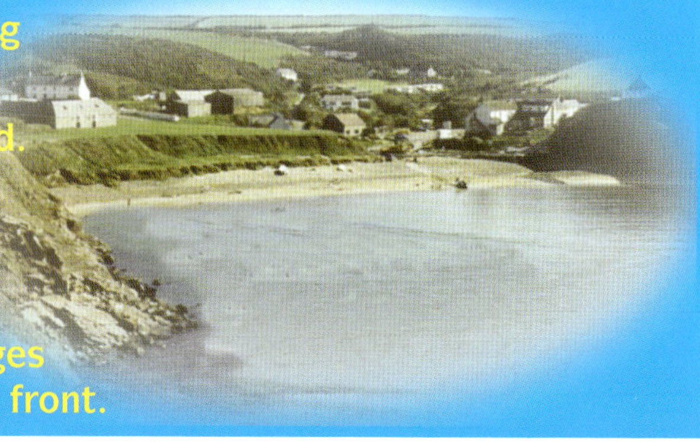

Cottages sleeping 2-8 persons.

All fully equipped.

Children and pets welcome.

Sympathetically converted cottages occupying beach front.

Wales

161

17th century farmhouse in the heart of Kilvert country, rural Radnorshire, only five miles from Hay-on-Wye the famous centre for secondhand books. You will find peace and tranquillity in this wonderful walking country. Within easy reach of the Brecon Beacons National Park, Herefordshire and even the Welsh coast. Two self-catering apartments; sleeping between two and eleven in comfort, which easily combine for a larger party. WTB ★★★

MRS E. BALLY, LANE FARM, PAINSCASTLE, BUILTH WELLS LD2 3JS
Tel & Fax: 01497 851605 • e-mail: lanefarm@onetel.com
www.lane-farm.co.uk

Comfortable self-catering holiday bungalows sleeping 2-7 near Trearddur's lovely beaches. Indoor heated swimming pool, licensed club, tennis court. Local, beautiful headland walks, fishing, golf and horse riding. Ideal location to explore Anglesey and the North Wales coast; near Holyhead.

TREARDDUR HOLIDAY BUNGALOWS
LON ISALLT, TREARDDUR BAY ANGLESEY LL65 2UP

Tel: 01407 860494 • *trearholiday@btconnect.com* • *www.holiday-bungalows.co.uk*

Betws-y-Coed, North Wales

Whitehall Cottage

This cosy cottage, formerly part of a vicarage, has been sympathetically renovated and is warm and welcoming. Situated in the small hamlet of Kinnerton in the picturesque Radnor Valley, it is an ideal centre for touring Mid Wales, its beautiful borderland, South Shropshire and Herefordshire.

The lounge, with inglenook fireplace and wood burner has a comfortable suite, television/video and a supply of books, plus a folder of tourist information.

The well equipped kitchen/diner has an electric cooker, microwave, dishwasher, washing machine and fridge. Ground floor cloakroom.

Two light, airy, prettily furnished bedrooms – a twin and a double. Central heating throughout, linen and towels provided, cot and high chair available.

Private sun-trap garden, with wendy house and garden furniture, secure for children and pets, ample space for parking.

There are plenty of local pubs and restaurants for an evening out, and New Radnor [3 miles] has a village shop and post office. Activities nearby include pony trekking, paragliding, walking, birdwatching.

MRS R. L. JONES, UPPER HOUSE, KINNERTON, NEAR PRESTEIGNE, POWYS LD8 2PE
• Tel: 01547 560207 •

163

LEIGHTON BUZZARD RAILWAY
Page's Park Station, Billington Road,
Leighton Buzzard, Bedfordshire LU7 4TN
Tel: 01525 373888
e-mail: station@lbngrs.org.uk
www.buzzrail.co.uk

One FREE adult/child with full-fare adult ticket
Valid 14/3/2010 - 31/10/2010

FHG READERS' OFFER 2010 · K·U·P·E·R·A·R·D

NOT TO BE USED IN CONJUNCTION WITH ANY OTHER OFFER

BEKONSCOT MODEL VILLAGE & RAILWAY
Warwick Road, Beaconsfield,
Buckinghamshire HP9 2PL
Tel: 01494 672919
e-mail: info@bekonscot.co.uk
www.bekonscot.co.uk

One child FREE when accompanied by full-paying adult
Valid February to October 2010

FHG READERS' OFFER 2010 · K·U·P·E·R·A·R·D

NOT TO BE USED IN CONJUNCTION WITH ANY OTHER OFFER

BUCKINGHAMSHIRE RAILWAY CENTRE
Quainton Road Station, Quainton,
Aylesbury HP22 4BY
Tel: 01296 655720
e-mail: office@bucksrailcentre.org
www.bucksrailcentre.org

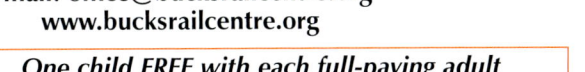

One child FREE with each full-paying adult
Not valid for Special Events or Day Out with Thomas

FHG READERS' OFFER 2010 · K·U·P·E·R·A·R·D

NOT TO BE USED IN CONJUNCTION WITH ANY OTHER OFFER

THE RAPTOR FOUNDATION
The Heath, St Ives Road,
Woodhurst, Huntingdon, Cambs PE28 3BT
Tel: 01487 741140 • Fax: 01487 841140
e-mail: heleowl@aol.com
www.raptorfoundation.org.uk

TWO for the price of ONE
Valid until end 2010 (not Bank Holidays)

FHG READERS' OFFER 2010 · K·U·P·E·R·A·R·D

NOT TO BE USED IN CONJUNCTION WITH ANY OTHER OFFER

A 70-minute journey into the lost world of the English narrow gauge light railway. Features historic steam locomotives from many countries. **PETS MUST BE KEPT UNDER CONTROL AND NOT ALLOWED ON TRACKS**	**Open:** Sundays and Bank Holiday weekends 14 March to 31 October. Additional days in summer, and school holidays. **Directions:** on south side of Leighton Buzzard. Follow brown signs from town centre or A505/A4146 bypass.

FHG GUIDES, ABBEY MILL BUSINESS CENTRE, PAISLEY PA1 1TJ • www.holidayguides.com

Be a giant in a magical miniature world of make-believe depicting rural England in the 1930s. "A little piece of history that is forever England."	**Open:** 10am-5pm daily mid February to end October. **Directions:** Junction 16 M25, Junction 2 M40.

FHG GUIDES, ABBEY MILL BUSINESS CENTRE, PAISLEY PA1 1TJ • www.holidayguides.com

A working steam railway centre. Steam train rides, miniature railway rides, large collection of historic preserved steam locomotives, carriages and wagons.	**Open:** daily April to October 10.30am to 4.30pm. Variable programme - check website or call. **Directions:** off A41 Aylesbury to Bicester Road, 6 miles north west of Aylesbury.

FHG GUIDES, ABBEY MILL BUSINESS CENTRE, PAISLEY PA1 1TJ • www.holidayguides.com

Birds of Prey Centre offering audience participation in flying displays which are held 3 times daily. Tours, picnic area, gift shop, tearoom, craft shop.	**Open:** 10am-5pm all year except Christmas and New Year. **Directions:** follow brown tourist signs from B1040.

FHG GUIDES, ABBEY MILL BUSINESS CENTRE, PAISLEY PA1 1TJ • www.holidayguides.com

READERS' OFFER 2010

NENE VALLEY RAILWAY
Wansford Station, Stibbington,
Peterborough, Cambs PE8 6LR
Tel: 01780 784444
e-mail: nvrorg@nvr.org.uk
www.nvr.org.uk

One child FREE with each full paying adult.
Valid Jan. to end Oct. 2010 (excludes galas and pre-ticketed events)

NOT TO BE USED IN CONJUNCTION WITH ANY OTHER OFFER

READERS' OFFER 2010

ANSON ENGINE MUSEUM
Anson Road, Poynton,
Cheshire SK12 1TD
Tel: 01625 874426
e-mail: enquiry@enginemuseum.org
www.enginemuseum.org

Saturdays - 2 for 1 entry (when one of equal or greater value is purchased). Valid 12 April-30 Sept 2010

NOT TO BE USED IN CONJUNCTION WITH ANY OTHER OFFER

READERS' OFFER 2010

NATIONAL SEAL SANCTUARY
Gweek, Helston,
Cornwall TR12 6UG
Tel: 01326 221361
e-mail: seals@sealsanctuary.co.uk
www.sealsanctuary.co.uk

TWO for ONE - on purchase of another ticket of equal or greater value. Valid until December 2010.

NOT TO BE USED IN CONJUNCTION WITH ANY OTHER OFFER

READERS' OFFER 2010

LAPPA VALLEY RAILWAY
Benny Halt, St Newlyn East,
Newquay, Cornwall TR8 5LX
Tel: 01872 510317
e-mail: info@lappavalley.co.uk
www.lappavalley.co.uk

75p per person OFF up to a maximum of £3
Valid Easter to end October 2010.

NOT TO BE USED IN CONJUNCTION WITH ANY OTHER OFFER

Take a trip back in time on the delightful Nene Valley Railway with its heritage steam and diesel locomotives, There is a 7½ mile ride from Wansford to Peterborough via Yarwell, with shop, museum and excellent cafe at Wansford Station (free parking).	**Open:** please phone or see website for details. **Directions:** situated 4 miles north of Peterborough on the A1

FHG GUIDES, ABBEY MILL BUSINESS CENTRE, PAISLEY PA1 1TJ • www.holidayguides.com

As seen on TV, this multi award-winning attraction has a great deal to offer visitors. It houses the largest collection of engines in Europe, local history area, craft centre (bodging and smithy work), with changing exhibitions throughout the season.	**Open:** Easter Sunday until end October, Friday to Sunday and Bank Holidays, 10am to 5pm. **Directions:** approx 7 miles from J1 M60 and 9 miles J3 M60. Follow brown tourist signs from Poynton traffic lights.

FHG GUIDES, ABBEY MILL BUSINESS CENTRE, PAISLEY PA1 1TJ • www.holidayguides.com

Set on the beautiful Helford Estuary, the National Seal Sanctuary is Europe's busiest seal rescue centre. Every year the Sanctuary rescues and releases over 30 injured or abandoned seal pups and provides a refuge for those seals/sea lions unable to be returned to the wild.	**Open:** daily (except Christmas Day) from 10am. **Directions:** from A30 follow signs to Helston, then brown tourist signs to Seal Sanctuary.

FHG GUIDES, ABBEY MILL BUSINESS CENTRE, PAISLEY PA1 1TJ • www.holidayguides.com

Three miniature railways, plus leisure park with canoes, crazy golf, large children's play area with fort, brickpath maze, wooded walks (all inclusive). Dogs welcome (50p).	**Open:** Easter to end October **Directions:** follow brown tourist signs from A30 and A3075

FHG GUIDES, ABBEY MILL BUSINESS CENTRE, PAISLEY PA1 1TJ • www.holidayguides.com

THE BOND MUSEUM
Southey Hill, Keswick,
Cumbria CA12 5NR
Tel: 017687 74044
e-mail: thebondmuseum@aol.com
www.thebondmuseum.com

One FREE child with two paying adults.
Valid February to October 2010.

NOT TO BE USED IN CONJUNCTION WITH ANY OTHER OFFER

THE BEACON
West Strand, Whitehaven,
Cumbria CA28 7LY
Tel: 01946 592302 • Fax: 01946 598150
e-mail: thebeacon@copelandbc.gov.uk
www.thebeacon-whitehaven.co.uk

One FREE adult/concesssion when accompanied by one full paying
adult/concession. Under 16s free. Valid from Oct 2009 to end 2010.
Not valid for special events. Day tickets only.

NOT TO BE USED IN CONJUNCTION WITH ANY OTHER OFFER

CRICH TRAMWAY VILLAGE
Crich, Matlock
Derbyshire DE4 5DP
Tel: 01773 854321 • Fax: 01773 854320
e-mail: enquiry@tramway.co.uk
www.tramway.co.uk

One child FREE with every full-paying adult
Valid during 2010

NOT TO BE USED IN CONJUNCTION WITH ANY OTHER OFFER

THE MILKY WAY ADVENTURE PARK
The Milky Way, Clovelly,
Bideford, Devon EX39 5RY
Tel: 01237 431255
e-mail: info@themilkyway.co.uk
www.themilkyway.co.uk

10% discount on entrance charge.
Valid Easter to end October (not August).

NOT TO BE USED IN CONJUNCTION WITH ANY OTHER OFFER

For all "Bond" or car fans this is a must! Aston Martins, Lotus, even a T55 Russsian tank from the film "Goldeneye". Also cinema and shop.	**Open:** 10am to 5pm February to end October; weekends November and December. **Directions:** from Penrith (M6) take A66 to Keswick. Free parking.

FHG GUIDES, ABBEY MILL BUSINESS CENTRE, PAISLEY PA1 1TJ • www.holidayguides.com

The Beacon is the Copeland area's interactive museum, tracing the area's rich history, from as far back as prehistoric times to the modern day. Enjoy panoramic views of the Georgian town and harbour from the 4th floor viewing gallery. Art gallery, gift shop, restaurant. Fully accessible.	**Open:** open all year (excl. 24 26 Dec) Tuesday to Sunday, plus Monday Bank Holidays. **Directions:** enter Whitehaven from north or south on A595. Follow the town centre and brown museum signs; located on harbourside.

FHG GUIDES, ABBEY MILL BUSINESS CENTRE, PAISLEY PA1 1TJ • www.holidayguides.com

A superb family day out in the atmosphere of a bygone era. Explore the recreated period street and fascinating exhibitions. Unlimited tram rides are free with entry. Play areas, woodland walk and sculpture trail, shops, tea rooms, pub, restaurant and lots more.	**Open:** daily April to end October 10am to 5.30pm. **Directions:** eight miles from M1 Junction 28, follow brown and white signs for "Tramway Museum".

FHG GUIDES, ABBEY MILL BUSINESS CENTRE, PAISLEY PA1 1TJ • www.holidayguides.com

The day in the country that's out of this world! With 5 major rides and loads of great live shows. See Merlin from 'Britain's Got Talent' 5 days a week. All rides and shows included in entrance fee.	**Open:** 10.30am - 6pm. Check for winter opening hours. **Directions:** on the main A39 one mile from Clovelly.

FHG GUIDES, ABBEY MILL BUSINESS CENTRE, PAISLEY PA1 1TJ • www.holidayguides.com

THE BIG SHEEP
Abbotsham, Bideford,
North Devon EX39 5AP
Tel: 01237 472366 • Fax: 01237 477916
e-mail: info@thebigsheep.co.uk
www.thebigsheep.co.uk

FHG READERS' OFFER 2010

2 for 1 admission. Valid all year

NOT TO BE USED IN CONJUNCTION WITH ANY OTHER OFFER

DEVONSHIRE COLLECTION OF PERIOD COSTUME
Totnes Costume Museum,
Bogan House, 43 High Street,
Totnes,
Devon TQ9 5NP

FHG READERS' OFFER 2010

FREE child with a paying adult with voucher
Valid from Spring Bank Holiday to end of Sept 2010

NOT TO BE USED IN CONJUNCTION WITH ANY OTHER OFFER

WOODLANDS FAMILY THEME PARK
Blackawton, Dartmouth,
Devon TQ9 7DQ
Tel: 01803 712598 • Fax: 01803 712680
e-mail: fun@woodlandspark.com
www.woodlandspark.com

FHG READERS' OFFER 2010

12% discount off individual admission price.
No photocopies. Valid 26 March to 7 November 2010.

NOT TO BE USED IN CONJUNCTION WITH ANY OTHER OFFER

COMBE MARTIN WILDLIFE & DINOSAUR PARK
Higher Leigh, Combe Martin,
North Devon EX34 0NG
Tel: 01271 882486
e-mail: info@dinosaur-park.com
www.dinosaur-park.com

FHG READERS' OFFER 2010

One child FREE with two paying adults.
Valid February to November 2010

NOT TO BE USED IN CONJUNCTION WITH ANY OTHER OFFER

The best day of your holiday baa none! Sheep racing, dog and duck trialling, huge indoor playground, animal barn with pets' corner and lamb bottle feeding, train and tractor rides, and much more.

Open: 10am-6pm daily April to October. From Nov-March weekends and school holidays only. Please check opening times before visiting.

Directions: two miles west of Bideford, on the A39 Atlantic Highway. Look for the big flag.

FHG GUIDES, ABBEY MILL BUSINESS CENTRE, PAISLEY PA1 1TJ • www.holidayguides.com

---

Themed exhibition, changed annually, based in a Tudor house. Collection contains items of dress for women, men and children from 17th century to 1990s, from high fashion to everyday wear.

Open: Open from Spring Bank Holiday to end September. 11am to 5pm Tuesday to Friday.

Directions: centre of town, opposite Market Square. Mini bus up High Street stops outside.

FHG GUIDES, ABBEY MILL BUSINESS CENTRE, PAISLEY PA1 1TJ • www.holidayguides.com

---

A wide variety of rides, plus zoo and farm, makes a fantastic day out for all ages. Awesome indoor adventure centres, ball blasting arenas, mirror maze and soft play ensures wet days are fun. 16 family rides including white knuckle Swing Ship, electrifying Watercoasters, terrifying Toboggan Run, Superb Falconry Centre, Big Fun Farm, animals, tractor ride, weird and wonderful zoo creatures. An all-weather attraction.

Open: 26 March to 7 November 2010 open daily 9.30am. In winter open weekends and local school holidays.

Directions: 5 miles from Dartmouth on A3122. Follow brown tourist signs from A38.

FHG GUIDES, ABBEY MILL BUSINESS CENTRE, PAISLEY PA1 1TJ • www.holidayguides.com

---

*The home of the only full size animatronic T-Rex. Explore 26 acres of stunning gardens with cascading waterfalls, exotic birds and animals. Daily sea lion shows, falconry displays, lemur encounters, 3 magnificent lions, brass rubbing centre.
A great day out for all the family.*

Open: 10am to 5pm (last entry 3pm). February half term to 8th Nov.

Directions: take M5 to Junction 27. Go west along the A361 towards Barnstaple, turn right on to the A399, and then follow signs for Combe Martin and Ilfracombe.

FHG GUIDES, ABBEY MILL BUSINESS CENTRE, PAISLEY PA1 1TJ • www.holidayguides.com

|171|

DINOSAUR ISLE
Culver Parade, Sandown,
Isle of Wight PO36 8QA
Tel: 01983 404344 • Fax: 01983 407502
e-mail: dinosaur@iow.gov.uk
www.dinosaurisle.com

One child FREE when accompanied by full paying adult.
Valid from February to December 24th 2010.

NOT TO BE USED IN CONJUNCTION WITH ANY OTHER OFFER

ROMNEY, HYTHE & DYMCHURCH RAILWAY
New Romney Station,
New Romney,
Kent TN28 8PL
Tel: 01797 362353
www.rhdr.org.uk

Romney, Hythe & Dymchurch Railway

One child FREE with every two full paying adults.
Valid until end 2010 except on special event days.

NOT TO BE USED IN CONJUNCTION WITH ANY OTHER OFFER

CHISLEHURST CAVES
Old Hill, Chislehurst,
Kent BR7 5NL
Tel: 020 8467 3264 • Fax: 020 8295 0407
e-mail: info@chislehurstcaves.co.uk
www.chislehurstcaves.co.uk

FREE child entry with full paying adult.
Valid until end 2010 (not Bank Holiday weekends)

NOT TO BE USED IN CONJUNCTION WITH ANY OTHER OFFER

NATURELAND SEAL SANCTUARY
North Parade, Skegness
Lincolnshire PE25 1DB
Tel: 01754 764345
e-mail: info@skegnessnatureland.co.uk
www.skegnessnatureland.co.uk

One child admitted FREE when accompanied by full
paying adult on production of voucher. Valid to end 2010.

NOT TO BE USED IN CONJUNCTION WITH ANY OTHER OFFER

In a spectacular pterosaur-shaped building, watching over Sandown's Blue Flag beach, is Britain's first purpose-built dinosaur museum. Walk back through fossilised time and meet life-size model dinosaurs including an animated Neovenator.

Open: open all year except 24-26th December and Ist January (call for opening hours Jan/Feb).
Daily 10am-5pm (March-Oct), 10am-4pm (Nov-Feb).

Directions: on B3395 coastal road.

FHG GUIDES, ABBEY MILL BUSINESS CENTRE, PAISLEY PA1 1TJ • www.holidayguides.com

Heritage steam miniature railway and model exhibition. 27 miles round trip following the Kent coastline. The railway runs from Hythe, Dymchurch, New Romney, Romney Sands and Dungeness.

Open: 9.45am to 6pm.
Check website for details.

FHG GUIDES, ABBEY MILL BUSINESS CENTRE, PAISLEY PA1 1TJ • www.holidayguides.com

Miles of mystery and history beneath your feet! Grab a lantern and get ready for an amazing underground adventure. Your whole family can travel back in time as you explore this labyrinth of dark mysterious passageways. See the caves, church, Druid altar and more.

Open: Wed to Sun from 10am; last tour 4pm. Open daily during local school and Bank holidays (except Christmas). Entrance by guided tour only.

Directions: A222 between A20 and A21; at Chislehurst Station turn into Station Approach; turn right at end, then right again into Caveside Close.

FHG GUIDES, ABBEY MILL BUSINESS CENTRE, PAISLEY PA1 1TJ • www.holidayguides.com

A specialised collection of animals including seals, penguins, tropical birds and butterflies (April to October), reptiles, aquarium, pets' corner etc. Known worldwide for rescuing orphaned and injured seal pups and returning almost 600 back to the wild.

Open: daily except Christmas Day, Boxing Day and New Year's Day.

Directions: north end of Skegness seafront.

FHG GUIDES, ABBEY MILL BUSINESS CENTRE, PAISLEY PA1 1TJ • www.holidayguides.com

173

FHG KUPERARD
READERS' OFFER 2010

EXMOOR FALCONRY & ANIMAL FARM
Allerford, Near Porlock, Minehead,
Somerset TA24 8HJ
Tel: 01643 862816
e-mail: exmoor.falcon@virgin.net
www.exmoorfalconry.co.uk

*10% off entry to Falconry Centre
Valid during 2010*

NOT TO BE USED IN CONJUNCTION WITH ANY OTHER OFFER

FHG KUPERARD
READERS' OFFER 2010

THE NATIONAL HORSERACING MUSEUM
99 High Street,
Newmarket,
Suffolk CB8 8JH
Tel: 01638 667333
www.nhrm.co.uk

*One FREE adult or concession with on paying full price.
Valid Easter to end October 2010. Museum admission only.*

NOT TO BE USED IN CONJUNCTION WITH ANY OTHER OFFER

FHG KUPERARD
READERS' OFFER 2010

EASTON FARM PARK
Pound Corner, Easton, Woodbridge,
Suffolk IP13 0EQ
Tel: 01728 746475
e-mail: info@eastonfarmpark.co.uk
www.eastonfarmpark.co.uk

*One FREE child entry with a full paying adult
Only one voucher per group. Valid during 2010.*

NOT TO BE USED IN CONJUNCTION WITH ANY OTHER OFFER

FHG KUPERARD
READERS' OFFER 2010

PARADISE PARK
Avis Road, Newhaven,
East Sussex BN9 0DH
Tel: 01273 512123 • Fax: Fax: 01273 616005
e-mail: enquiries@paradisepark.co.uk
www.paradisepark.co.uk

*One child FREE with one full paying adult.
Valid January - end October 2010.*

NOT TO BE USED IN CONJUNCTION WITH ANY OTHER OFFER

Falconry centre with animals - flying displays, animal handling, feeding and bottle feeding - in 15th century NT farmyard setting on Exmoor. Also falconry and outdoor activities, hawk walks and riding.

Open: 10.30am to 5pm daily

Directions: A39 west of Minehead, turn right at Allerford, half a mile along lane on left.

FHG GUIDES, ABBEY MILL BUSINESS CENTRE, PAISLEY PA1 1TJ • www.holidayguides.com

Stories of racing, ride the horse simulator, or take a 'behind the scenes' tour of the training grounds and yards.

Open: Easter to end October, 7 days a week 11am to 5pm. Last admission 4pm.

Directions: on the High Street in the centre of Newmarket.

FHG GUIDES, ABBEY MILL BUSINESS CENTRE, PAISLEY PA1 1TJ • www.holidayguides.com

Family day out down on the farm, with activities for children every half hour (included in entry price). Indoor and outdoor play areas. Riverside cafe, gift shop. For more details visit the website.

Open: 10.30am-6pm daily March to September.

Directions: signposted from A12 in the direction of Framlingham.

FHG GUIDES, ABBEY MILL BUSINESS CENTRE, PAISLEY PA1 1TJ • www.holidayguides.com

Discover 'Planet Earth' for an unforgettable experience. A unique Museum of Life, Dinosaur Safari, beautiful Water Gardens with fish and wildfowl, plant houses, themed gardens, Heritage Trail, miniature railway. Playzone includes crazy golf and adventure play areas. Garden Centre and Terrace Cafe.

Open: 9am - 6pm daily except Christmas/Boxing Days.

Directions: signposted from A26 and A259.

FHG GUIDES, ABBEY MILL BUSINESS CENTRE, PAISLEY PA1 1TJ • www.holidayguides.com

175

FHG K·U·P·E·R·A·R·D
READERS' OFFER 2010

WORLD OF JAMES HERRIOT
23 Kirkgate, Thirsk,
North Yorkshire YO7 1PL
Tel: 01845 524234
Fax: 01845 525333
www.worldofjamesherriot.org

Admit TWO for the price of ONE (one voucher per transaction only). Valid until October 2010

NOT TO BE USED IN CONJUNCTION WITH ANY OTHER OFFER

FHG K·U·P·E·R·A·R·D
READERS' OFFER 2010

MUSEUM OF RAIL TRAVEL
Ingrow Railway Centre, Near Keighley,
West Yorkshire BD21 5AX
Tel: 01535 680425
e-mail: admin@vintagecarriagestrust.org
www.vintagecarriagestrust.org

*"ONE for ONE" free admission
Valid during 2010 except during special events (ring to check)*

NOT TO BE USED IN CONJUNCTION WITH ANY OTHER OFFER

FHG K·U·P·E·R·A·R·D
READERS' OFFER 2010

EUREKA! THE NATIONAL CHILDREN'S MUSEUM
Discovery Road, Halifax,
West Yorkshire HX1 2NE
Tel: 01422 330069 • Fax: 01422 398490
e-mail: info@eureka.org.uk
www.eureka.org.uk

*One FREE child on purchase of full price adult ticket
Valid from 1/10/09 to 31/12/10. Excludes groups. Promo Code 243*

NOT TO BE USED IN CONJUNCTION WITH ANY OTHER OFFER

FHG K·U·P·E·R·A·R·D
READERS' OFFER 2010

THE GRASSIC GIBBON CENTRE
Arbuthnott, Laurencekirk,
Aberdeenshire AB30 1PB
Tel: 01561 361668
e-mail: lgginfo@grassicgibbon.com
www.grassicgibbon.com

TWO for the price of ONE entry to exhibition (based on full adult rate only). Valid during 2010 (not groups)

NOT TO BE USED IN CONJUNCTION WITH ANY OTHER OFFER

Visit James Herriot's original house recreated as it was in the 1940s. Television sets used in the series 'All Creatures Great and Small'. There is a children's interactive gallery with life-size model farm animals and three rooms dedicated to the history of veterinary medicine.

Open: daily. Easter-Oct 10am-5pm; Nov-Easter 11am to 4pm

Directions: follow signs off A1 or A19 to Thirsk, then A168, off Thirsk market place

FHG GUIDES, ABBEY MILL BUSINESS CENTRE, PAISLEY PA1 1TJ • www.holidayguides.com

A fascinating display of railway carriages and a wide range of railway items telling the story of rail travel over the years.

ALL PETS MUST BE KEPT ON LEADS

Open: daily 11am to 4.30pm

Directions: approximately one mile from Keighley on A629 Halifax road. Follow brown tourist signs

FHG GUIDES, ABBEY MILL BUSINESS CENTRE, PAISLEY PA1 1TJ • www.holidayguides.com

As the UK's National Children's Museum, Eureka! is a place where children play to learn and grown-ups learn to play.

Open: daily except 24-26 December, 10am to 5pm

Directions: leave M62 at J24 for Halifax. Take A629 to town centre, following brown tourist signs.

FHG GUIDES, ABBEY MILL BUSINESS CENTRE, PAISLEY PA1 1TJ • www.holidayguides.com

Visitor Centre dedicated to the much-loved Scottish writer Lewis Grassic Gibbon. Exhibition, cafe, gift shop. Outdoor children's play area. Disabled access throughout.

Open: daily March to October 10am to 4.30pm. Groups by appointment including evenings.

Directions: on the B967, accessible and signposted from both A90 and A92.

FHG GUIDES, ABBEY MILL BUSINESS CENTRE, PAISLEY PA1 1TJ • www.holidayguides.com

177

READERS' OFFER 2010

SCOTTISH MARITIME MUSEUM
Harbourside, Irvine,
Ayrshire KA12 8QE
Tel: 01294 278283
Fax: 01294 313211
www.scottishmaritimemuseum.org

TWO for the price of ONE
Valid from April to October 2010

NOT TO BE USED IN CONJUNCTION WITH ANY OTHER OFFER

READERS' OFFER 2010

GALLOWAY WILDLIFE CONSERVATION PARK
Lochfergus Plantation, Kirkcudbright,
Dumfries & Galloway DG6 4XX
Tel & Fax: 01557 331645
e-mail: info@gallowaywildlife.co.uk
www.gallowaywildlife.co.uk

One FREE child or Senior Citizen with two full paying adults.
Valid Feb - Nov 2010 (not Easter weekend and Bank Holidays)

NOT TO BE USED IN CONJUNCTION WITH ANY OTHER OFFER

READERS' OFFER 2010

BO'NESS & KINNEIL RAILWAY
Bo'ness Station, Union Street,
Bo'ness, West Lothian EH51 9AQ
Tel: 01506 822298
e-mail: enquiries.railway@srps.org.uk
www.srps.org.uk

FREE child train fare with one paying adult/concession. Valid March-Oct 2010. Not Days Out with Thomas or Santa Steam trains

NOT TO BE USED IN CONJUNCTION WITH ANY OTHER OFFER

READERS' OFFER 2010

MYRETON MOTOR MUSEUM
Aberlady,
East Lothian EH32 0PZ
Tel: 01875 870288
www.myretonmotormuseum.co.uk

MYRETON MOTOR MUSEUM

One child FREE with each paying adult
Valid during 2010

NOT TO BE USED IN CONJUNCTION WITH ANY OTHER OFFER

Scotland's seafaring heritage is among the world's richest and you can relive the heyday of Scottish shipping at the Maritime Museum.	**Open:** 1st April to 31st October - 10am-5pm **Directions:** situated on Irvine harbourside and only a 10 minute walk from Irvine train station.

FHG GUIDES, ABBEY MILL BUSINESS CENTRE, PAISLEY PA1 1TJ • www.holidayguides.com

The wild animal conservation centre of Southern Scotland. A varied collection of over 150 animals from all over the world can be seen within natural woodland settings. Picnic areas, cafe/gift shop, outdoor play area, woodland walks, close animal encounters.	**Open:** 10am to dusk 1st February to 30 November. **Directions:** follow brown tourist signs from A75; one mile from Kirkcudbright on the B727.

FHG GUIDES, ABBEY MILL BUSINESS CENTRE, PAISLEY PA1 1TJ • www.holidayguides.com

Steam and heritage diesel passenger trains from Bo'ness to Birkhill for guided tours of Birkhill fireclay mines. Explore the history of Scotland's railways in the Scottish Railway Exhibition. Coffee shop and souvenir shop.	**Open:** weekends Easter to October, daily July and August. See website for dates and timetables. **Directions:** in the town of Bo'ness. Leave M9 at Junction 3 or 5, then follow brown tourist signs.

FHG GUIDES, ABBEY MILL BUSINESS CENTRE, PAISLEY PA1 1TJ • www.holidayguides.com

On show is a large collection, from 1899, of cars, bicycles, motor cycles and commercials. There is also a large collection of period advertising, posters and enamel signs.	**Open:** March-Oct: open daily 10.30am to 4.30pm. Nov-Feb: weekends 11am to 3pm or by special appointment. **Directions:** off A198 near Aberlady. Two miles from A1.

FHG GUIDES, ABBEY MILL BUSINESS CENTRE, PAISLEY PA1 1TJ • www.holidayguides.com

179

FHG
·K·U·P·E·R·A·R·D·
READERS' OFFER 2010

BRITISH GOLF MUSEUM
Bruce Embankment, St Andrews,
Fife KY16 9AB
Tel: 01334 460046 • Fax: 01334 460064
e-mail: judychance@randa.org
www.britishgolfmuseum.co.uk

*10% off price of admission (one per customer).
Valid during 2010.*

NOT TO BE USED IN CONJUNCTION WITH ANY OTHER OFFER

FHG
·K·U·P·E·R·A·R·D·
READERS' OFFER 2010

SCOTTISH DEER CENTRE
Cupar,
Fife KY15 4NQ
Tel: 01337 810391
e-mail: info@tsdc.co.uk
www.tsdc.co.uk

One child FREE with one full paying adult on production of voucher. Not valid during December.

NOT TO BE USED IN CONJUNCTION WITH ANY OTHER OFFER

FHG
·K·U·P·E·R·A·R·D·
READERS' OFFER 2010

LOCH NESS CENTRE & EXHIBITION EXPERIENCE
Drumnadrochit, Loch Ness,
Inverness-shire IV63 6TU
Tel: 01456 450573 • 01456 450770
www.lochness.com

'2 for the price of 1' entry to the world famous Exhibition Centre. Valid during 2010.

NOT TO BE USED IN CONJUNCTION WITH ANY OTHER OFFER

FHG
·K·U·P·E·R·A·R·D·
READERS' OFFER 2010

NATIONAL CYCLE COLLECTION
Automobile Palace, Temple Street,
Llandrindod Wells, Powys LD1 5DL
Tel: 01597 825531
e-mail: cycle.museum@powys.org.uk
www.cyclemuseum.org.uk

*TWO for the price of ONE
Valid during 2010 except Special Event days*

NOT TO BE USED IN CONJUNCTION WITH ANY OTHER OFFER

The 5-Star British Golf Museum explores 500 years of golfing history using exciting interactives and diverse displays. A visit here makes the perfect break from playing golf.

Open: Mon-Sat 9.30am-5pm, Sun 10am-4pm. Closed Christmas and New Year periods.

Directions: opposite the Old Course in St Andrews.

FHG GUIDES, ABBEY MILL BUSINESS CENTRE, PAISLEY PA1 1TJ • www.holidayguides.com

---

55-acre park with 10 species of deer from around the world. Guided tours, trailer rides, treetop walkway, children's adventure playground and picnic area. Other animals include wolves, foxes, otters and a bird of prey centre.

Open: 10am to 5pm daily except Christmas Day and New Year's Day.

Directions: A91 south of Cupar. Take J9 M90 from the north, J8 from the south.

FHG GUIDES, ABBEY MILL BUSINESS CENTRE, PAISLEY PA1 1TJ • www.holidayguides.com

---

VisitScotland 5-Star Visitor Attraction, described by Scottish Natural Heritage as "a portal to the unique natural phenomenon that is Loch Ness'. Cafe and restaurant on site with large shopping complex and cruises on Loch Ness.

Open: all year except Christmas Day.

Directions: directly on A82 trunk road, 12 miles south of Inverness.

FHG GUIDES, ABBEY MILL BUSINESS CENTRE, PAISLEY PA1 1TJ • www.holidayguides.com

---

Journey through the lanes of cycle history and see bicycles from Boneshakers and Penny Farthings up to modern Raleigh cycles. Over 250 machines on display

PETS MUST BE KEPT ON LEADS

Open: 1st March to 1st November daily 10am onwards.

Directions: brown signs to car park. Town centre attraction.

FHG GUIDES, ABBEY MILL BUSINESS CENTRE, PAISLEY PA1 1TJ • www.holidayguides.com

Index of towns and sections

Aberaeron	WALES
Aberporth	WALES
Abington	SCOTLAND
Ambleside	NORTH WEST
Ashbourne	MIDLANDS
Ashford	KENT
Auchtermuchty	SCOTLAND
Aviemore	SCOTLAND
Avoch	SCOTLAND
Axminster	SOUTH DEVON
Bacton-on-Sea	EAST OF ENGLAND
Barmouth	WALES
Barnstaple	NORTH DEVON
Beaminster	HAMPSHIRE & DORSET
Betws-y-Coed	WALES
Bideford	NORTH DEVON
Bishop Auckland	NORTH EAST
Blue Anchor	SOMERSET & WILTSHIRE
Bodmin	CORNWALL
Bournemouth	HAMPSHIRE & DORSET
Bridgwater	SOMERSET & WILTSHIRE
Brixham	SOUTH DEVON
Broad Haven	WALES
Broadwoodwidger	SOUTH DEVON
Bude	CORNWALL
Burwell	EAST OF ENGLAND
Buxton	MIDLANDS
Caernarfon	WALES
Callander	SCOTLAND
Carrbridge	SCOTLAND
Charmouth	HAMPSHIRE & DORSET
Clitheroe	NORTH WEST
Cockermouth	NORTH WEST
Colwyn Bay	WALES
Crackington Haven	CORNWALL
Dalbeattie	SCOTLAND
Dartmouth	SOUTH DEVON
Devizes	SOMERSET & WILTSHIRE
Dorchester	HAMPSHIRE & DORSET
Dunkeld	SCOTLAND
Dunsford	NORTH DEVON
Dunster	SOMERSET & WILTSHIRE
Eskdale	NORTH WEST
Exmouth	SOUTH DEVON
Falmouth	CORNWALL
Fowey	CORNWALL
Framlingham	EAST OF ENGLAND
Harlech	WALES
Harrogate	NORTH EAST
Haverfordwest	WALES
Hawkshead	NORTH WEST
Hayle	CORNWALL
Hayling Island	HAMPSHIRE & DORSET
Hay-on-Wye	WALES
Hingham	EAST OF ENGLAND
Ilfracombe	NORTH DEVON
Inveraray	SCOTLAND
Kessingland	EAST OF ENGLAND
Kingsbridge	SOUTH DEVON
Kingston-upon-Thames	LONDON & HOME COUNTIES
Lairg	SCOTLAND
Langport	SOMERSET & WILTSHIRE
Launceston	CORNWALL
Leek	MIDLANDS
Leven	SCOTLAND
Liskeard	CORNWALL
Little Torrington	NORTH DEVON
Lizard Peninsula	CORNWALL
Loch Lomond	SCOTLAND
Lochinver	SCOTLAND
London	LONDON & HOME COUNTIES
Looe	CORNWALL
Lowestoft	EAST OF ENGLAND
Lulworth Cove	HAMPSHIRE & DORSET
Lynton	NORTH DEVON
Lytham St Annes	NORTH WEST
Maidstone	KENT
Marazion	CORNWALL
Millom	NORTH WEST
Minehead	SOMERSET & WILTSHIRE
Modbury	SOUTH DEVON
Moretonhampstead	SOUTH DEVON
Newquay	CORNWALL
Okehampton	NORTH DEVON
Orkney Islands	SCOTLAND
Padstow	CORNWALL
Poole	HAMPSHIRE & DORSET
Portland	HAMPSHIRE & DORSET
Portnahaven	SCOTLAND
Portwrinkle	CORNWALL
Presteigne	WALES
St Annes on Sea	NORTH WEST
St Ives	CORNWALL
St Tudy	CORNWALL
Seaton	SOUTH DEVON
Sherbōrne	HAMPSHIRE & DORSET
South Molton	NORTH DEVON
Stanton by Bridge	MIDLANDS
Stow-on-the-Wold	MIDLANDS
Stratford-upon-Avon	MIDLANDS
Studland Bay	HAMPSHIRE & DORSET
Taunton	SOMERSET & WILTSHIRE
Tenbury Wells	MIDLANDS
Totland	ISLE OF WIGHT
Totnes	SOUTH DEVON
Trearddur Bay	WALES
Truro	CORNWALL
Tunbridge Wells	KENT
Ventnor	ISLE OF WIGHT
Watchet	SOMERSET & WILTSHIRE
Westbury	SOMERSET & WILTSHIRE
Weymouth	HAMPSHIRE & DORSET
Whitby	NORTH EAST
Wimborne	HAMPSHIRE & DORSET
Windermere	NORTH WEST
Woolacombe	NORTH DEVON

Ratings & Awards

For the first time ever the AA, VisitBritain, VisitScotland, and the Wales Tourist Board will use a single method of assessing and rating serviced accommodation. Irrespective of which organisation inspects an establishment the rating awarded will be the same, using a common set of standards, giving a clear guide of what to expect. The RAC is no longer operating an Hotel inspection and accreditation business.

Accommodation Standards: Star Grading Scheme

Using a scale of 1-5 stars the objective quality ratings give a clear indication of accommodation standard, cleanliness, ambience, hospitality, service and food, This shows the full range of standards suitable for every budget and preference, and allows visitors to distinguish between the quality of accommodation and facilities on offer in different establishments. All types of board and self-catering accommodation are covered, including hotels, B&Bs, holiday parks, campus accommodation, hostels, caravans and camping, and boats.

VisitBritain and the regional tourist boards, enjoyEngland.com, VisitScotland and VisitWales, and the AA have full details of the grading system on their websites

The more stars, the higher level of quality

★★★★★
exceptional quality, with a degree of luxury

★★★★
excellent standard throughout

★★★
very good level of quality and comfort

★★
good quality, well presented and well run

★
acceptable quality; simple, practical, no frills

National Accessible Scheme

If you have particular mobility, visual or hearing needs, look out for the National Accessible Scheme. You can be confident of finding accommodation or attractions that meet your needs by looking for the following symbols.

 Typically suitable for a person with sufficient mobility to climb a flight of steps but would benefit from fixtures and fittings to aid balance

 Typically suitable for a person with restricted walking ability and for those that may need to use a wheelchair some of the time and can negotiate a maximum of three steps

 Typically suitable for a person who depends on the use of a wheelchair and transfers unaided to and from the wheelchair in a seated position. This person may be an independent traveller

 Typically suitable for a person who depends on the use of a wheelchair in a seated position. This person also requires personal or mechanical assistance (eg carer, hoist).

Other FHG titles for 2010

FHG Guides Ltd have a large range of attractive holiday accommodation guides for all kinds of holiday opportunities throughout Britain. They also make useful gifts at any time of year. Our guides are available in most bookshops and larger newsagents but we will be happy to post you a copy direct if you have any difficulty. POST FREE for addresses in the UK. We will also post abroad but have to charge separately for post or freight.

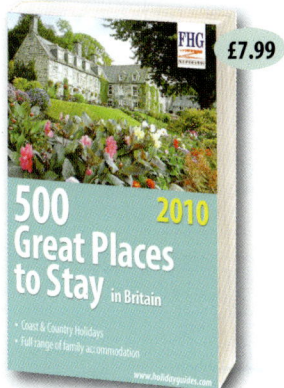 £7.99

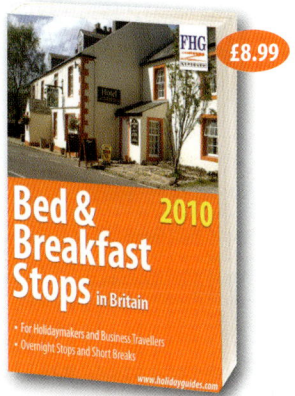 £8.99

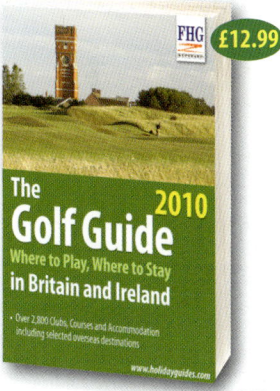 £12.99

500 Great Places to Stay in Britain
• Coast & Country Holidays
• Full range of family accommodation

Bed & Breakfast Stops in Britain
• For holidaymakers and business travellers
• Overnight stops and Short Breaks

The Golf Guide
Where to play, Where to stay.
• Over 2800 golf courses in Britain with convenient accommodation.
• Holiday Golf in France, Portugal, Spain, USA and Thailand.

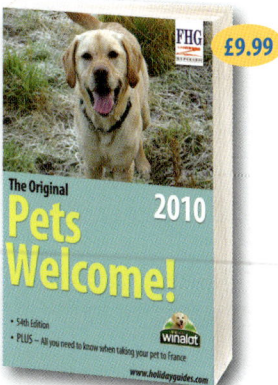 £9.99

 £6.99

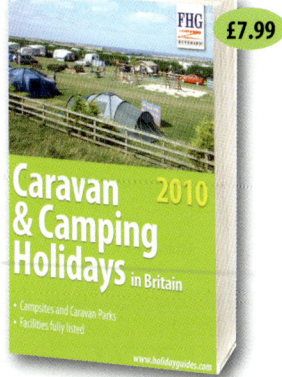 £7.99

The Original Pets Welcome!
• The bestselling guide to holidays for pets and their owners

Country Hotels of Britain
• Hotels with Conference, Leisure and Wedding Facilities

Caravan & Camping Holidays in Britain
• Campsites and Caravan parks
• Facilities fully listed

 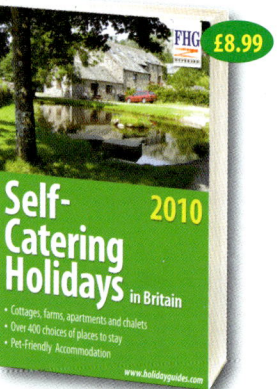 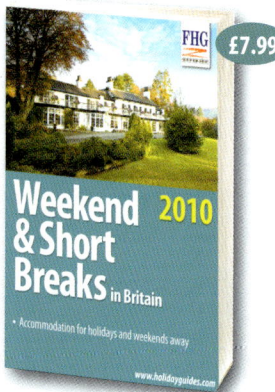

Pubs & Inns
of Britain
• Including Dog-friendly Pubs
• Accommodation, food and traditional good cheer

Self-Catering Holidays
in Britain
• Cottages, farms, apartments and chalets
• Over 400 places to stay
• Pet-Friendly accommodation

Weekend & Short Breaks
in Britain
• Accommodation for holidays and weekends away

Tick your choice above and send your order and payment to

**FHG Guides Ltd. Abbey Mill Business Centre
Seedhill, Paisley, Scotland PA1 1TJ
TEL: 0141- 887 0428 • FAX: 0141- 889 7204
e-mail: admin@fhguides.co.uk**

Deduct 10% for 2/3 titles or copies; 20% for 4 or more.

Send to: NAME ....

            ADDRESS ....

            ....

            ....

            POST CODE ....

I enclose Cheque/Postal Order for £ ....

            SIGNATURE ....DATE ....

Please complete the following to help us improve the service we provide.
How did you find out about our guides?:

☐ Press   ☐ Magazines   ☐ TV/Radio   ☐ Family/Friend   ☐ Other